W9-AMS-744

# Voices on the Cross

Compiled and Edited by K. Neill Foster
and Douglas B. Wicks

*Cling to the Cross!*

*Gal 2:20*

*God bless you*

*Pastor Paul J. Li GMDN*

**CHRISTIAN PUBLICATIONS, INC.**
CAMP HILL, PENNSYLVANIA

## *Dedication*

This book is dedicated to the ministry and memory of
*Dr. Richard W. Bailey*, a preacher of the cross.

**CHRISTIAN PUBLICATIONS, INC.**
www.christianpublications.com

*Faithful, biblical publishing since 1883*

*Voices on the Cross*
ISBN: 0-87509-966-1
© 2002 by Christian Publications, Inc.
02  03  04  05  06    5  4  3  2  1

# *Contents*

# The Fourfold Gospel and the Cross

# *Foreword*

The "preaching of the cross!" It is a phrase that sets my soul to singing. I confess that I love preaching that focuses upon and lifts up the cross of Jesus Christ.

It seems also that the Apostle Paul felt much the same when he exulted, "For the [preaching] of the cross is foolishness to those who are perishing, but to us who are being saved it is the power of God" (1 Corinthians 1:18).

My mentoring in the preaching of the cross has come from three sources.

The first was through a friend—Duane Morscheck. Duane was an Alliance evangelist much loved over many years in many churches. When he came to our church, I wondered what kind of man this was! I soon found out, and when we extended two weeks of meetings to three we all knew something special was going on.

It wasn't long until I was taking him from house to house so that he could explain the Spirit-filled life and help our folks to enter in. His exposition of the Book of Romans was for me. I learned that if we through the Spirit do make dead the deeds of the body, we will live (Romans 8:13). How wonderfully liberating that was. And many of our people were filled with the Holy Spirit.

Are you surprised that Duane died on a Good Friday? I suppose that if God had offered him a day on which to die, he would have chosen the day of the cross.

The second mentoring impulse came not from a person but from an event—the preaching of the cross and the experiencing of the cross as exhibited in revival. Specifically, I am referring to a revival in Canada in 1971-1972.

Hundreds of people were being crucified with Christ. It was a spreading flame among God's people across the land. What is sometimes thought to be an obscure theological nuance—preaching the cross of Jesus Christ and becoming crucified with Him—became a holy fire, front and center. I am a marked man ever since.

The third influence of power in my life was Dr. Richard W. Bailey, man of God and preacher of the cross. I once listened to him preach at Colorado Springs—at the New Workers' Seminar that I attended as the leader of Christian Publications. As he developed his theme on the cross, I found myself saying "Amen" and "Amen" again and again. And I do not belong by habit in the "Amen" corner. Perhaps I am exaggerating, but it seems to me in recall that scores of times in that single Richard Bailey sermon on the cross, I simply could not resist the flow of "Amen" joy and affirmation.

So, I have become a preacher of the cross myself. These lines and these messages are sent forth with a passion for the cross! May the hundreds and thousands who read these lines be crucified with Christ. Let us hurry to embrace the cross and die upon it. The Holy Spirit has come into the world to make it happen. By faith, as always, the cross becomes oh so real.

K. Neill Foster
President
February 2002

# *The Glory of the Cross*

# The Old Cross and the New

*by A.W. Tozer*

All unannounced and mostly undetected there has come in modern times a new cross into popular evangelical circles. It is like the old cross, but different: the likenesses are superficial; the differences, fundamental.

From this new cross has sprung a new philosophy of the Christian life, and from that new philosophy has come a new evangelical technique—a new type of meeting and a new kind of preaching. This new evangelism employs the same language as the old, but its content is not the same and its emphasis not as before.

The old cross would have no truck with the world. For Adam's proud flesh it meant the end of the journey. It carried into effect the sentence imposed by the law of Sinai. The new cross is not opposed to the human race; rather, it is a friendly pal and, if understood aright, it is the source of oceans of good clean fun and innocent enjoyment. It lets Adam live without interference. His life motivation is unchanged; he still lives for his own pleasure, only now he takes delight in singing choruses and watching religious movies instead of singing bawdy songs and drinking hard liquor. The accent is still on enjoyment, though the fun is now on a higher place morally if not intellectually.

The new cross encourages a new entirely different evangelistic approach. The evangelist does not demand abnegation of the old life before a new life can be received. He preaches not contrasts but similarities. He seeks to key into public interest by showing that Christianity makes no unpleasant demands; rather, it offers the same thing the world does, only on a higher level. Whatever the sin-mad world happens to be clamoring after at the moment is cleverly shown to be the very thing the gospel offers, only the religious product is better.

The new cross does not slay the sinner, it redirects him. It gears him into a cleaner and jollier way of living and saves his self-respect. To the self-assertive it says, "Come and assert yourself for Christ." To the egotist it says, "Come and do your boasting in the Lord." To the thrill seeker it says, "Come and enjoy the thrill of Christian fellowship." The Christian message is slanted in the direction of the current vogue in order to make it acceptable to the public.

The philosophy back of this kind of thing may be sincere but its sincerity does not save it from being false. It is false because it is blind. It misses completely the whole meaning of the cross.

The old cross is a symbol of death. It stands for the abrupt, violent end of a human being. The man in Roman times who took up his cross and started down the road had already said good-bye to his friends. He was not coming back. He was going out to have it ended.

The cross made no compromise, modified nothing, spared nothing; it slew all of the man, completely and for good. It did not try to keep on good terms with its victim. It struck cruel and hard, and when it had finished its work, the man was no more.

The race of Adam is under a death sentence. There is no commutation and no escape. God cannot approve any of the fruits of sin, however innocent they may appear or beautiful to the eyes of men. God salvages the individual by liquidating him and then raising him again to newness of life.

That evangelism which draws friendly parallels between the ways of God and the ways of men is false to the Bible and cruel to the souls of its hearers. The faith of Christ does not parallel the world, it intersects it. In coming to Christ we do not bring our old life up onto a higher place; we leave it at the cross. The corn of wheat must fall into the ground and die.

We who preach the gospel must not think of ourselves as public relations agents sent to establish good will between Christ and the world. We must not imagine ourselves commissioned to make Christ acceptable to big business, the press, the world of sports or modern education. We are not diplomats but prophets, and our message is not a compromise but an ultimatum.

God offers life, but not an improved old life. The life He offers is life out of death. It stands always on the far side of the cross. Whoever would possess it must pass under the rod. He must repudiate himself and concur in God's just sentence against him.

What does this mean to the individual, the condemned man who would find life in Christ Jesus? How can this theology be translated into life? Simply, he must repent and believe. He must forsake his sins and then go on to forsake himself. Let him cover nothing, defend nothing, excuse nothing. Let him not seek to make terms with God, but let him bow his head before the stroke of God's stern displeasures and acknowledge himself worthy to die.

Having done this let him gaze with simple trust upon the risen Savior, and from Him will come life and rebirth and cleansing and power. The cross that ended the earthly life of Jesus now puts an end to the sinner; and the power that raised Christ from the dead now raises him to a new life along with Christ.

To any who may object to this or count it merely a narrow and private view of truth, let me say God has set His hallmark of approval upon this message from Paul's day to the present. Whether stated in these exact words or not, this has been the content of all preaching that has brought life and power to the world through the centuries. The mystics, the reformers, the revivalists have put their emphasis here, and signs and wonders and mighty operations of the Holy Ghost gave witness to God's approval.

Dare we, the heirs of such a legacy of power, tamper with the truth? Dare we with our stubby pencils erase the lines of the blueprint or alter the pattern shown us in the Mount? May God forbid. Let us preach the old cross and we will know the old power.

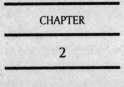

## CHAPTER
## 2

# Let the Cross Be Our Glory!

*by Peter N. Nanfelt*

**H**ave you ever stopped to realize what a common sight the symbol of the cross is in our society? Given the growing anti-Christian bias today, one would think that the cross would be something of an anathema.

But there it is hanging on chains around the necks of some of the most seedy and irreligious characters who appear regularly on TV screens and in popular movies. One of the star Major League Baseball players comes to bat with a gold cross dangling from his ear. We frequently see crosses dangling from rearview mirrors in many cars.

In the religious world, of course, we expect to see the cross. One of the most amazing sights I have ever seen is the evening skyline of Seoul, Korea, dotted with thousands of red neon-lit crosses. Many in our country were moved at the sight of multiple wooden crosses on the hillside overlooking Columbine High School in Colorado after the massacre there.

On top of Vail Mountain, outside of Denver here in Colorado, is a small amphitheater where services are held regularly. Worshipers look reverently across an enormous valley to a 14,000-foot mountain called the Mount of the

Holy Cross where, even late into the summer, white snow lies in deep ravines forming the shape of the cross on the face of the massive granite wall.

But does the average person, religious or otherwise, have any idea what the cross symbolizes? Perhaps to certain individuals it is something of a good-luck charm. Maybe there are others who genuinely believe that the cross, in whatever form, carries some sort of innate spiritual power—a religious relic, as it were. But it seems that to the majority of our society the cross has no more meaning than the Nike "swoosh."

If ever The Christian and Missionary Alliance hopes to be a movement of Great Commission Christians, the cross must have a prominent place in our lives and in our preaching.

Often we talk about cross-bearing, and that is an extremely important aspect of our Christian walk. Joseph Stowell, the president of Moody Bible Institute, has observed,

> Our willingness to pay the price of a cross is the pivotal issue of being a fully devoted follower. If I refuse crosses, then I cannot be a follower; if I follow, then crosses are inevitable. The cost is measured in some of the more prized currency in our lives—comfort, convenience, health, wealth, fulfillment, and self protection. Cross-bearing is an essential component of Christian discipleship.

But there is something that must precede cross-bearing. It is "cross-embracing." It is one thing to hang a cross on a chain around our necks. It is quite another to embrace all that the cross of Christ stands for. As ministers of the gospel, are we talking enough about what the cross really means? Are we expecting people who never have embraced the message of the cross to bear the shame of the cross? This simply will not work.

It is not easy to preach about the cross today. To speak about the cross, we need to talk about hell, and hell never has been a very popular subject. In our society, to speak of hell is not only unpopular, but it is also considered politically incorrect.

In the January 31, 2000, issue of *U.S. News and World Report*, Jeffery Shaler wrote that hell used to be pictured as a literal place of fiery torment, an "outer darkness" with "weeping and gnashing of teeth." Modern hell is much more benign, embarrassing and even cartoonish. Shaler quotes one observer as saying, "Hell has disappeared and no one noticed."

A massive book was recently published entitled, *Who's Who in Hell*, which seems to be a lighthearted spoof of the whole idea that there is such a place.

The reality today is that more people claim to believe in hell than they did fifty years ago. Could it be that the subject we are trying so hard to avoid is the very issue people are inwardly yearning to hear about? John MacArthur recently referred to a survey of evangelical seminary students that revealed that nearly half (forty-six percent) felt preaching about hell to unbelievers is in poor taste.

What a tragedy! As the songwriter has said, we are to "let the cross be our glory, and the Lord be our song."

Christ's sacrifice of Himself on the cross frees people from the bondage and burden of sin that drags them inexorably into a dark and painful eternity. Most people, at least in the private moments of their lives, recognize that they carry this sin burden and desperately seek a release from its penalty.

Fourteen years ago the refuse of a city—orange peels, bottles, newspapers, aluminum foil, chicken bones, tin cans, old shoes, and the like—were carted off to an incinerator in Philadelphia. It was intended that the ashes would somehow be trucked into oblivion, but it didn't happen that way.

The 15,000 tons of ash were loaded on a ship for disposal. For years the ship roamed the earth seeking to deposit its load somewhere: the Bahamas, Puerto Rico, the Dominican Republic, Honduras, Guinea-Bissau, the Netherlands Antilles and Haiti. It eventually went to Senegal, Yugoslavia, Sri Lanka, Indonesia and the Philippines.

Several times the ship changed its name, changed its registry and flew the flag of different countries. It made no difference. There was no acceptable place to discard the toxic waste that filled its cavernous hold. Today, fourteen years from the time the load of ash left Philadelphia, a portion of it remains on a barge off the coast of Florida. And it waits.

People are waiting to hear how they can be freed from the burden of sin. They carry it around, not publishing the fact that they have it, but never forgetting it's there, deep inside them. They try everything to discard it. They change their appearance, work on their personality, move to a different neighborhood.

But the sin question never is resolved. Understandably, they don't want to talk about hell, and they desperately try to moderate the vivid descriptions of it that Jesus gave. Even the noted Bible scholar, John Stott, has decided that hell must be something less than eternal torment. He expresses the view that, certainly, God is more loving than to condemn people to such a future.

Stott's perspective is shared by many. From a personal standpoint I must say that nothing has so blessed my heart this past year than a refocusing on the wonder of God's grace. The fact that we can do nothing to make God love us any more, nor can we do anything to make God love us any less, is an incredible truth.

Proclaiming the reality of hell does not diminish God's grace. The fact that Christ bore the punishment we deserve, the agony of the cross and separation from the Father, only serves to underscore the magnitude of His grace! Yes, "let the cross be our glory, let the Lord be our song."

If we believe the words of Jesus who spoke in such unequivocal terms about eternal punishment, and if we believe that the preaching of the cross is the only answer to the sin problem that people wrestle with every day, shouldn't we be preaching more about the cross? Paul wrote, "God was pleased through the foolishness of what was preached to save those who believe" (1 Corinthians 1:21).

Let's unashamedly invite people to embrace the cross as the only way to deal with the reality of sin and hell. And let's vigorously proclaim the cross as the only hope of heaven.

As a movement of Great Commission Christians, let's glory in the cross of Christ!

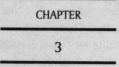

# The Cross of Jesus Christ and a Multiplied Harvest

*by Donald A. Wiggins*

What subject subdues a conversation or quiets a room more quickly than death? An awkward pause occurs before the conversation shifts to something acceptable.

To soften the sharp edge of death's finality, euphemisms are used in homes, hospitals and even the homilies at funerals. Family and friends appreciate such assuagement, but it cannot remove the stark reality that death produces grief, loss and a list of hard questions. Does death ever produce anything pleasant?

According to Jesus, yes. He spoke of an infinitely better crop of fruit from a different principle at work in death. The week leading Him to Calvary starts with an event all four Gospel writers record. Crowds of pilgrims on the way to Jerusalem for Passover take palm branches and hail Jesus as King when He passes by. Others already in the city go out to join the cheering crowd.

John writes that some God-fearing Greeks are in Jerusalem, also to worship, and they ask to see Jesus. Philip and Andrew bring the request to Jesus. Curiously, John does not say whether the Greeks gain an audience. But He does report Jesus' words to the disciples, perhaps overheard by the crowds around them:

> "The hour has come for the Son of Man to be glorified. I tell you the truth, unless a kernel of wheat falls to the ground and dies, it remains only a single seed. But if it dies, it produces many seeds. The man who loves his life will lose it, while the man who hates his life in this world will keep it for eternal life. Whoever serves me must follow me; and where I am, my servant also will be. My Father will honor the one who serves me." (John 12:23-26)

The hour of Jesus' death was at hand. In a not so veiled reference to His impending crucifixion, He stated a simple principle. If a wheat kernel does not fall into the ground and die, it remains one seed. But if it dies, it produces a harvest.

His words remind me of an incredible harvest scene in southwest Nebraska. On a perfect July Sunday morning the two-lane road climbed a long hill to the country church where I was to preach. The summit revealed a breath-taking vista. Thousands of acres of amber wheat fields stretched before me in a full circle to the horizon.

Where did all that ripe grain come from? From seeds, of course. The only way to produce the harvest was by planting seeds and letting them die in the ground. Wheat plants sprang up and yielded mature kernels for reaping.

But suppose the previous fall the farmers decided, "It would be a waste to let these seeds die in the ground.

Let's just keep them in our seed bins." How ludicrous that sounds, because saving the seed would have netted no harvest at all. The seeds must give their life to produce greater life.

In the same way, Jesus had to die like a kernel of wheat. Just as one kernel produces many seeds, His one death yields a great harvest. This spiritual principle of the dying seed is introduced by the ultimate conqueror of death. Jesus intends to populate heaven with waves of citizens around His throne, like that Nebraska landscape, as far as the eye can see. I can't help but wonder if among them will stand the Greeks who wanted to talk to Jesus.

## Remarkable Paradox in Jesus' Words

Life comes through death, Jesus says. In fact, a harvest of life comes through death. That doesn't seem to make sense. After all, millions of dollars are spent every day trying to put off physical death and prolong life. But Jesus contradicts the instinct to preserve life. In exchange for His one death, life comes forth—not just one new life, but a mega-harvest of many lives. Augustine said of Jesus: "He Himself was the grain that had to die, and be *multiplied*; to suffer death through the unbelief of the Jews, and to be *multiplied* in the faith of many nations" (emphasis added).

## The Way to Life

Death doesn't seem to be the way to life, but in fact it is! Death is the only pathway by which the gospel multiplies among many nations. Jesus was willing to walk the road to Calvary, to die there and be buried in the ground, in order to produce a multiplied harvest of changed lives among the nations.

Don't think for a minute that death was easy for Jesus. He considered asking for a rescue: "Now my heart is troubled, and what shall I say? 'Father, save me from this hour'?" (John 12:27). But He refused: " 'No, it was for this very reason I came to this hour. Father, glorify your name!' Then a voice came from heaven, 'I have glorified it, and will glorify it again' " (12:27-28).

Jesus understood the awful, blessed paradox—through His death many would receive life! So He embraced the horrible consequences that lay ahead.

## Jesus Applies the Principle to His Disciples

"The man who loves his life will lose it, while the man who hates his life in this world will keep it for eternal life" (12:25).

Jesus offers His followers a choice. It is an either/or decision with no middle ground. Love your life and you lose it (literally, "are destroying it"). Hate your life in this world and you gain it for eternity. This is the choice that confronts Him. Having decided to lay down His life, the call is to follow Him down the same path He chose.

"Whoever serves me must follow me; and where I am, my servant also will be. My Father will honor the one who serves me" (12:26).

To those who choose the way of death, He offers a bright promise: "Where I am, my servant also will be. My Father will honor the one who serves me" (12:26). Being where Jesus is means death. It means hating one's own life by comparison to loving Him. But even if every-

13

thing in this life is lost, far more will be gained in eternity, for the Father will honor those servants who follow the Master into death.

## Application

If multiplied life comes from death, it impacts the follower of Jesus in several significant ways. Some questions may suggest how.

*If death was the pathway to life for Jesus and His first followers, why would it be any different for those who follow Him now?*

In death, Jesus gave up everything—self-determination, self-will, personal rights, even for a while His fellowship with the Father. Is it fair to expect that we should suffer a similar death? If so, all the ugly forms of the self-life in us must die—pride, cherished ambitions, personal rights, desire for recognition and power and position.

To that death list add all confidence in our own power and strength and every vain thought that we can help out God. And what about reliance on our own strategies and plans for ministry? That, too, must die. For the sake of following Jesus without reservation, it is necessary to lay down *everything* of value, especially life itself.

Not long ago, I dined with a group of Vietnamese pastors. Three of them were captured in their homeland after 1975 for preaching the gospel of Jesus Christ. These men endured a total of twenty-one years as prisoners for their faith and only later escaped to pastor again in America. They were the survivors; many more pastors lost their lives in the same prisons.

If God were to permit physical suffering in the United States, would He find such courage among pastors and church leaders? Or if He does not call us to die for the gospel, would He find servants willing to murder self-will and pride? As one *still* learning to die daily, the question is not for others; it is for me. What needs to die in order to follow Jesus all the way?

*If life is the product of death, what life-giving ministry does God have for you?*

We not only die, but we also rise with Christ so that He can produce life through us in others. Most followers I know are satisfied to spend most of their time with their Christian friends. But to be life-givers, we need intentional contact with those who do not know Christ. That responsibility cannot be passed off to someone else. It gets uncomfortable when someone asks, "Can you name five friends who are still far from God?" or "When did you last give a clear witness for Christ?" If there is hesitation, it's time to get intentional.

*Since death brings multiplied life, then what multiplying ministry does God have for you?*

Because Jesus died, a mega-harvest of grain will be gathered from all over the world into the Father's storehouse. Jesus desires to produce not just a little of that grain through each of us. He intends to reap a multiplied harvest.

One of the biggest hindrances, though, is the prevailing view among Christians that one must be particularly well-trained to participate in the harvest. God does not despise formal preparation, but He invites all followers to become multipliers.

Despite a lack of formal Bible training, the famous evangelist Billy Sunday asked to be ordained. Approval by the church would prove his orthodoxy and help him overcome dismissals that he was just an ex-professional baseball player. Since his wife was a Presbyterian, he submitted himself to examination in 1903 by the Chicago Presbytery.

To most of the questions on theology and church history he replied, "That's too deep for me" and "I'll have to pass that up." After several embarrassing minutes, a sympathizer on the ordination board moved that the remainder of the exam be waived. "God has used him to win more souls to Christ than all of us combined and must have ordained him long before we ever thought of it." In an exceptional stroke of wisdom, the rest agreed and passed him

God wants to multiply fruit through every follower of Jesus—multiplying disciples, leaders and churches. If more "average" Christians grasped the principle of multiplication, an incredible harvest would result.

## Conclusion

What an awesome call God has put on our lives. None of us feels adequate for the responsibility. And, of course, we are not. Only in Christ's mighty resurrected power are we made adequate to become life-giving servants.

The living Lord addresses us at three points—dying, giving life and multiplying the harvest. The harvest is worth whatever it costs us to say *yes* to Him. And at the end is the Father's favor.

What is the next step for churches and individual disciples who say yes? Consider this. Tommy Lasorda, the former Los Angeles Dodgers manager, was quoted in the *Denver Post* on June 19, 2000:

> You have players today who just want to hit home runs. They don't play the game the way it's supposed to be played, manufacturing runs, hitting the ball to the other side. They don't care about that. When we played, we played for the name on the front of the shirt, not the name on the back.

The team's name, not the player's name, is most important. Nothing less than a total agreement in Jesus' name is required to bring in the harvest.

*The Reach of Missions*

# The Cross of Jesus Christ and the Missionary Mandate

*by Stephen K. Bailey*

I n a world where the primary pursuit is personal convenience at any cost, the ideas of sacrifice and obligation are not likely to gain popular appeal. Yet at the end of the world's empty pursuit of happiness two questions remain: "Where is power located?" and "Who am I?" I want to reflect on these two questions within the framework of a postmodern worldview, the cross of Jesus Christ and the Christian obligation to communicate the gospel across boundaries (missions) in light of a core postmodern value.

Most of us in the West now live within the paradigm of postmodernism. Many people have preached and written about the evils associated with this. But I am convinced that there were as many ways to obey and disobey God in the paradigm of the Enlightenment as there are now within the postmodern paradigm. Postmodern thinking is here, and it is important that Christians learn to think and authentically testify to the gospel within it.

There have been many attempts to define postmodernism. For the purposes of this article I will limit my discussion to what is arguably the core of postmodernism. This core is located in a fundamental shift from an emphasis on observable, objective reality to an emphasis on experiential, subjective reality. It used to be that seminaries urged students to focus on *being* before the *doing* of Christian ministry. Today, Peter Wagner argues that for the most part ministry experience (i.e., doing) should define theological understanding (i.e., being). Not everyone comes to this focus on subjectivity from the perspective that Wagner does, but more and more Christians are starting from the subjective experience of relationship as a basis for working out their understanding of their faith.

For those of us used to the objectivity of the Enlightenment there may be a degree of discomfort with this shift—at least until we realize that our own spiritual roots in the Alliance can be traced back to this same kind of paradigm in A.B. Simpson's ministry. Like the Apostle Paul, Simpson allowed his theology to be shaped by the experience of his relationship with Jesus Christ. Wagner points out that in spite of Paul's thorough rabbinical training, he did not understand the Scriptures until he met Jesus face-to-face on the road to Damascus. Whether or not you buy into the postmodern critique of knowledge, Christians need to realize that a saving knowledge of God is dependent upon a personal, relationship with Jesus Christ. But what does this have to do with the two questions raised previously, the cross and missions?

It is important to note that Paul did not simply preach *any* kind of relationship with *any* kind of Christ. He preached a relationship with Christ crucified (1 Corinthians 1:23), which requires that we die with Christ and to the basic principles of this world (Galatians 2:20) in order that we might live with Christ (Romans 6:8). But what are the basic principles of this world that we must die to? In asking this question (which every one one of us asks in one way or another) we identify ourselves with the expert in the law who asked Jesus, "What must I do to inherit eternal life?" The answer is to love the Lord our God with all our heart, soul, strength and mind, and to love our neighbor as ourselves (Luke 10:27). Still trying to cling to the basic principles of this world we then ask, "Yes, but who is my neighbor?" The basic principles of this world come together in obtaining power to pursue my own good. The principle of the cross is to set aside power in order to seek the welfare of others.

Power is a central concern for people because they are inclined to seek their own good before the good of others. This is the basic principle of the world. This theme is beautifully portrayed in J.R.R. Tolkien's series, *The Lord of the Rings*. In this trilogy the one ultimate ring of power could only be destroyed by someone willing to give it up.

God the Father laid aside His supreme power to enter our world in Jesus Christ, who obediently died the death of a slave. Jesus did this in order to redeem our lives from the sin of seeking our own good outside of relationship with the Father. In dying on our behalf He modeled living on behalf of others (Philippians 2:4-11) and established the ethic of the kingdom of God. So in answer to the question, "Where is power?" Christians answer, "It is found in the cross of Christ where power is laid aside on behalf of others."

We come now to the second question, "Who am I?" and the missionary mandate. The cross of Christ designates our identity and mandates our partnership with God in His mission in the world. We have seen that the cross of Christ boldly set power aside for the sake of others and that those who follow Christ are also called to live and die on behalf of others. But why must we do this?

The gospel teaches us that contrary to our culture's pursuit of personal autonomy, we were made for life in community. In a prayer before His crucifixion, Jesus prayed to the Father "that all of them may be one, . . . just as you are in me and I am in you. May they also be in us so that the world may believe that you have sent me" (John 17:21).

In the world of the Enlightenment it was common for us to think of ourselves as separate, individual, autonomous beings, each with our own destiny to seek. But the postmodern world has one thing right. Humans are interdependent social beings. Everything we do and say impacts others and what others do impacts us as well. In a similar way, God exists in the community of the Trinity and created us to live in community. This fact helps us to better understand the cross and the ethic it established. In Christ, the cross obligates us to live on behalf of others because we belong to them, and they belong to us and to God.

In becoming one of the people of God, the question, "Who am I?" fades into insignificance. In the household of faith, who I am is defined by my relationship with Christ. My identity is also defined by my relationship and obligation to others. My identity in Christ and in His Church leaves me with what Paul called an inescapable "debt" to all those who are still where I once was—outside of the family of God.

Most of us think of family as a safe place to come home to. Home and family are meant to be places of comfort and intimacy. Strong families cherish their time together and even tend to avoid the intrusion of outsiders on their time together. Strong families also recognize their obligations to one another. But *healthy* families also recognize their responsibility to include outsiders in their fellowship because they realize that those outside the home are really extended family.

The tragic thing about God's family is that not everyone has come home yet. The good news is that God is on a mission to bring home as many as possible. God is even willing to abandon home for a time in order to find the others (Luke 15:4). As part of His family we are obligated to each other, to our extended family outside the church and to the deep desire of God to bring all our brothers and sisters home (1 Corinthians 9:16).

Learning to live on behalf of others requires that we put an end to pursuing our own interests, and, in a similar way, joining the mission of God in the world requires that we leave the comfort of home. The cross and mission are both about putting our identity aside for a time in order to take up the condition of others as a means to identifying with their situation. It would seem so much easier if we could just send them a letter with the information they need. Some Christians even today fall into the trap of thinking that what the world needs is the right information. From this standpoint literature and radio seem to be adequate for the job. Both literature and radio have important roles to play, but the long practice of the Alliance to send people into other societies to share Jesus Christ is grounded in the experience of our own relationship with Christ crucified. Christ crucified is the power of right relationships with God and with each other. It is a message of relationship, and it takes people to communicate it.

The cross and missions are also about crossing boundaries. Have you noticed how different people are outside the family of God? It would be so much easier if they would act, talk and look more like us. The first Christians in Jerusalem thought so. Acts 10 tells us the story of how God helped Peter understand that God did not require Gentiles to become like Jews in order to be followers of Christ. The gospel needed to cross the boundary line of the church in Jerusalem in order to reach the Gentiles.

In this postmodern world it seems more and more difficult to discern who belongs to the church and who does not. In the West, the once clearly defined boundary markers that set apart God's people from the people "of the world" seem to have been moved during the night. It used to be that we could know "our own" just by looking at them.

It used to be that if a man wore an earring to church we knew that, best case scenario, it was an opportunity to witness to some lost soul and, worst case scenario, that our ushers were probably competent to deal with the would-be thief. Today the man wearing the earring might be the Sunday morning guest speaker, and we feel relieved if he hasn't yet tattooed some exposed part of his body.

I suspect that the disorientation we feel in regard to the changing symbolism of our culture is not too unlike the feelings Peter experienced in Acts 10. In that vision God revealed to him that Gentiles—those people whose very presence could make a Jew ritually unclean—were now to be *welcomed* into the very midst of God's people.

I find it interesting that while Paul earned the title "missionary to the Gentiles," it was Peter who received the vision that revealed to the Early Church the full scope of God's mission. Perhaps this was because Peter, not Paul, needed to be pushed across the Jewish Christian boundary line. It was on the rock of Peter's life that Christ declared that He would build His church (Matthew 16:18).

Peter was a gatekeeper. He was at the center of power on the "Board of Trustees" in Jerusalem. The Board of Trustees in the Early Church occasionally met to deal with things like what kinds of things Gentiles should be allowed to eat at church potluck dinners. "Should we let them eat meat from animals that have been strangled, or meat with blood in it, or meat sacrificed to idols?" (Acts 15).

It seems almost comical that after the Jerusalem Board carefully worked out the rules of conformity for Gentile converts that they asked Paul to announce the new policy to all the Gentile churches. It was probably a bad decision on their part because when Paul arrived in Corinth he realized that the Board still didn't have it right. So Paul in effect said to the Corinthian Christians, "By the way, about

27

the Board's decision on meat, well . . . if it doesn't bother your conscience, forget about it and just give thanks to God for the food and enjoy" (1 Corinthians 10:25).

Church historian and former missionary, Andrew Walls, asks this question: "What would the Church have looked like had Peter failed to take the vision from God seriously?" He suggests that had Peter decided the vision had nothing to do with crossing the cultural and social boundaries to share Jesus, then at best the Church would have become a rather insignificant sect within Judaism. At worst the Church would have died out with the disciples. But Peter did take the vision seriously. In fact, he summed up the meaning of that vision with these words, "God has shown me that I should not call any man impure or unclean" (Acts 10:28).

Basically because of this conviction the gospel began to cross boundaries with the Church's blessing, and you and I, and millions more, speaking a thousand different languages, have all come to know Jesus as Lord. I like the way that Charles Van Engen defines mission. He says, "Mission is what happens on the boundary line between the people of God and the world." Mission is about crossing boundaries and removing barriers so that people may encounter the living Christ in their midst. Of course, this means living on behalf of others, too; otherwise, we would never leave home.

As I share this vision of mission with people, I often see them grow uncomfortable. We don't naturally want to move outside the boundaries of our group. Groups and family give us a sense of belonging and help define our identity. Social scientists can demonstrate to you that around the world people don't like it when you mess with the boundary lines of their identity. We are no different.

Standing on, or crossing, the boundary lines that define who we are feels dangerous, and we are not sure of those who wander around that boundary zone. But did you ever consider the boundary God crossed in order to meet us face-to-face in the Person of Jesus? Read the second chapter of Philippians with that thought in mind.

Paul writes in Galatians 3:28, "There is neither Jew nor Greek, slave nor free, male nor female, for you are all one in Christ Jesus." These social categories—Jew-Greek, slave-free, male-female—represented the three fundamental social divisions within Roman society in Paul's day. They were what separated people from one another in the world *and also in the church*. In contrast, participation in the life of the cross led Paul into a mission that required that he let the pursuit of his own good die in order to "become all things to all men so that by all possible means [he] might save some" (1 Corinthians 9:22).

Today we live in a time when things are not what they used to be. It looks dangerous outside the family of God. Like Tolkien's hobbits in the Shire we long for the comfort of the easy chair before the fireplaces in our homes. We forget what dangers and sufferings were endured for us by Christ in order to bring us home. We want to pretend that if we leave the front door unlocked for those who are interested that we have done all we can, forgetting the infinite obligation we are under. Christ bids us leave the comfort of the familiar to join in the search for lost men and women with whom we are forever related. They are our brothers and sisters. Can there be rest before they are found?

As we cross these boundary lines into the world we feel a sense of danger, which is only human. But when we feel this danger, do we turn back to our safe havens and the security of our past identity, or do we press ahead across every barrier that stands between us and the millions that surround us in North America, and the billions that fill our planet?

The cross's power is in the call to lay power aside on behalf of others. One of the implications of this is that we will put aside the pursuit of our own interests in order to join God's mission in the world. His mission requires that we cross the boundaries of our identity, which we found in the cross, so that by all possible means some might know Jesus as we know Him.

# The Cross of Jesus Christ for the World

*by Arnold L. Cook*

I n 519 B.C., King Darius I of Persia crucified 3,500 political enemies in Babylon. Initially, executioners used a stake upon which to impale criminals. But by the time of Christ a crossbar had been added—sometimes carried by the condemned individual and fastened to the upright. God in His infinite wisdom chose this, the most ignominious form of death, as the timeless world symbol and signature of Christianity.

In his book, *Hitler's Cross*, Erwin Lutzer reminds us how the cross of Jesus Christ has been compromised for political agendas:

> Church leaders throughout Germany allowed the swastika (form of the Greek cross) a prominent place alongside the Christian cross in their sanctuaries. Nationalistic pride replaced the call of God to purity, and with few exceptions, the German church looked away while Adolf Hitler implemented his "final solution" to the Jewish problem.

Tragically this sacred symbol has suffered both at the hands of friends and foes. In the fourth century, the well-intentioned Roman Emperor Constantine, having triumphed in battle under the sign of the cross, made Christianity the state religion. This opened the door to multitudes of nominal Christians to become part of the official Church.

Some of the darkest pages of Christian history record the infamous "Christian" crusades against the Muslims during the eleventh and twelfth centuries. Some eight centuries later, in the latter part of the twentieth century, a group of Christians wearing T-shirts bearing the words "we're sorry" retraced the crusade routes in an attempt at generational reconciliation. They asked forgiveness for the brutalities committed against Muslims by their ancestors in the name of the cross.

How does the cross of Christ relate to this world? Initially the cross strikes the world as being a big religious "scandal." But then the Holy Spirit supernaturally draws the same sceptical world, one by one, to repentance and saving faith in the Christ of the cross. The once-irrelevant cross is transformed into the powerful cross of radical conversion. In the next phase the cross comes full circle as the crucified and resurrected Christ through His Church moves powerfully against the "god of this world" with an army of radical disciples. He delivers on His promise: "I will build my church." He continues today as His Church through His empowered people lays siege to the very "gates of Hades" (Matthew 16:18).

The above analysis of the cross of Christ has been summarized also in this way: The cross takes us out of the world through the new birth. Then the cross takes the world out of us through sanctification. And, finally, this same cross sends us back into the world through evangelism and missions.

## "The Message of the Cross Is Foolishness" to the World (1 Corinthians 1:18)

When God chose the cross as His ultimate expression of His love for the world, He ignored everything of a worldly nature. The cross was "a stumbling block to Jews" (1:23) who expected a triumphant Messiah who would liberate them from their Roman oppressors. For the Gentiles, especially the philosophical Greeks, the idea of "good news" being even remotely linked to a "cross" constituted unadulterated nonsense.

After twenty centuries of creative reconfigurations of dozens of crosses, such as the French, the Celtic, the Greek, the Crusader, the English Canterbury, the Bethlehem, the Scotch, etc., any cross still remains a stumbling block to the unbelieving world. Some critics even designate Christianity as a slaughterhouse religion or a bloody faith.

The late twentieth-century Western Evangelical Church has worked ingeniously attempting to give the "old rugged cross" a face-lift. A.W. Tozer calls their product "a new cross." He contrasts it with the "old cross":

> The new cross does not slay the sinner, it redirects him. It gears him into a cleaner and jollier way of living and saves his self-respect. To the self assertive it says, "Come and assert yourself

for Christ." To the egotist it says, "Come and do your boasting in the Lord," to the thrill-seeker it says, "Come enjoy the thrill of Christian fellowship." . . .

The old cross is a symbol of death; it stands for the abrupt, violent end of a human being. The man in Roman times, who took up his cross and started down the road, had already said good-bye to his friends. He was not coming back. He was not going out to have his life redirected. He was going out to have it ended. The cross made no compromise, modified nothing, spared nothing; it slew all the man completely and for good.

The unbelieving Jews and Gentiles of Paul's day can be forgiven for their lack of understanding of the cross. In the same context Paul describes such unregenerate people as "natural men" who do not understand the things of the Spirit of God, "for they are foolishness" to them (1 Corinthians 2:14). Still later he refers to the Corinthians as "worldly," thinking and "acting like mere men" (3:3). This aptly describes those well-meaning but misguided carnal believers who with worldly wisdom have created the "user-friendly cross."

## "But to Us Who Are Being Saved [the Message of the Cross] Is the Power of God" (1 Corinthians 1:18)

Why did God bypass the scholars, the philosophers and the wisdom of the Greeks? In the immediate context Paul gives two reasons: God is a *transcendent* God, far above all earthly wisdom. "For the foolishness of God is wiser than man's wisdom, and the weakness of God is stronger than man's strength" (1:25). Then Paul adds, God is also a *jealous* God, and His glory He will not give to another (Deuteronomy 4:24). "Therefore, as it is written: 'Let him who boasts boast in the Lord' " (1 Corinthians 1:31).

I was a first-term missionary witnessing to Roman Catholic students. Based upon my missiological training I knew I needed to contextualize the gospel. These young people had been taught that Protestantism was splintered. So I found just the tract to counter that misconception titled: "What Evangelicals Believe in All the World." I was the first Protestant they had met, so they often raised the name of Martin Luther, the first Protestant, who left the Catholic Church to marry a nun. "Right?" This inevitably triggered animated discussions about which church was the true church.

After several months of this approach, I finally woke up. I realized that though I was winning most of the debates, I was losing all my contacts and leading no one to Christ! The Spirit of God, the master evangelist, caught my full attention through this Scripture:

> The god of this age has blinded the minds of unbelievers, so that they cannot see the light of the gospel of the glory of Christ, who is the image of God. For *we do not preach ourselves, but Jesus Christ as Lord, and ourselves as your servants for Jesus' sake*. (2 Corinthians 4:4-5, emphasis added)

"Thank You, Lord," I prayed. "I've been preaching 'ourselves as evangelicals' and not Christ." Using "words of human wisdom" I had emptied the cross of Christ of its power (1 Corinthians 1:17). I converted to Paul's stance immediately: "For I resolved to know nothing . . . except Jesus Christ and him crucified" (2:2). Then God began bringing into His kingdom converted students. This early corrective strategy harmonized my missionary ministry with Paul's basic thesis: *"For the foolishness of God is wiser than man's wisdom, and the weakness of God is stronger than man's strength"* (1:25, emphasis added).

The cross is God's centerpiece, manifesting to the watching world His love and power to every generation. Here are but a few demonstrations of His love and power among the nations of this world:

- He created the world out of nothing (Genesis 1:1).
- He established His special people miraculously through Abraham and Sarah (Genesis 21).
- He controlled the flow of history, using questionable individuals to bring Christ through the tribe of Judah (Matthew 1:1-17).
- He sent His Son into a precarious setting; e.g., teenage parents; birth in a stable; the death threat of Herod; etc. (Luke 2).
- Christ chose twelve ordinary men, one who betrayed Him and the rest who deserted Him at His death (Luke 22-23).
- He used a "weak" first-century church, without real estate, buildings, influence or technology to impact their century more effectively than any church has done since.

- He preserved a flickering gospel light throughout the Dark Ages.
- He raised up reformers, revival and missionary movements in the sixteenth, seventeenth, eighteenth and nineteenth centuries, launching world evangelization.
- In the greatest of missionary centuries, the twentieth, He intervened with power where human wisdom had failed:
  1. He transformed what appeared like a "wild fire" movement, Azusa Street 1906, into the largest Protestant movement today.
  2. He took what missionaries wrote off as a mission disaster in China in 1948, when communism moved in, and transformed it into the greatest church-growth story in twenty centuries.
  3. He stepped into a desperate situation for Indonesia in the mid-1960s. This largest of Muslim countries was destined to fall to communism. But the graves they dug to bury missionaries were filled by communists as God reversed the coup.
  4. He has built His Church around the world. Consider this amazing growth: In A.D. 100 there were 360 non-Christians to every Christian. By A.D. 1000 it was down to 220. Then by the fifteenth-century Reformation the ratio was 69 to 1 Christian. By 1900 it was 27, and by A.D. 2000 it was reduced to 8 to 1.

Missiologist Ralph Winter asks the question, "Is there any other trend lasting 2,000 years of documented history which is as unshakeably true and unquestionably significant?" The mere existence of the Christian Church is a major miracle. But this Church, with the cross of Jesus, is marching toward the culmination of history. It is established in all the continents, in almost every country and is moving rapidly into the final unreached people groups of every nation.

With thanksgiving we declare again with Paul: "For the message of the cross is foolishness to those who are perishing, but to us who are being saved *it is the power of God*" (1 Corinthians 1:18, emphasis added).

*The Power of the Cross*

| CHAPTER | **Ministering the Cross of Jesus Christ** |
|:---:|:---|
| 6 | |

*by Rockwell L. Dillaman*

There are three forces with which we must contend—the world, the flesh and the devil. Of these, the most dangerous is the flesh, for it constitutes the enemy within. The world and the devil attack from without. They rely on the flesh for access. If the flesh is brought into submission, that access is denied.

The Apostle Paul warns, "The flesh sets its desire against the Spirit, and the Spirit against the flesh; for these are in opposition to one another, so that you may not do the things that you please" (Galatians 5:17, NASB). To what was he referring? While "flesh" as a spiritual dynamic is not defined, its activities are certainly described. Based upon those descriptions I would suggest the following definition: "Flesh" is human intellect, will and emotion acting independently of God.

By this definition all manner of activity can be fleshly—including religious activity. If that reality is not recognized, we stand to lose anointing and forfeit power and effectiveness. We will produce a great commotion but not fulfill the Great Commission. History tells the sad tale of churches and denominations that became bogged down in intellectual emphasis, emotional fervor or reliance upon force of will. These soon held to a form of godliness but lacked power.

Paul's writings in Colossians and elsewhere indicate that while we are no longer obligated to obey the flesh, we are obligated to resist it. But any form of resistance will not do. Some forms of resistance only serve to strengthen the flesh. The only resistance that is effective comes by way of cross-bearing, a discipline that doesn't occur unless one understands the process.

Pioneer missionary Mabel Francis discovered this reality while serving with the Alliance in Japan. Finding herself struggling with pride, defensiveness and a host of other attitudes that weakened her ministry, she stated,

> I had thought that when I was cleansed by the blood of Jesus and filled with the Holy Spirit all the self-life was taken away. He showed me that His method for dealing with the self-life was not just cleansing, but crucifixion. I said, "Lord Jesus, I don't know how to die. Teach me to die."

Inspired and informed by Mabel's testimony, I echoed her petition during the second year of my first pastorate. In the days that followed, God granted me a fresh insight into the relevance of Matthew 10:38: "And he who does not take his cross and follow after Me is not worthy of Me" (NASB). "Worthy" doesn't make sense if it means "deserving." We are never deserving of God and His grace. But another inference of the word is "conforming to the pattern of." That definition, inserted into the verse, gives new meaning. It indicates the cross was not only a place where God made provision for my need but also laid a pattern for my life. Philippians 3:10 captures this concept when it speaks of "being conformed to His death" (NASB).

There are two crosses in the life of the believer. The first is the cross of Christ where He died once for all to change my standing before God. The other is *my* cross; it is a place of ongoing self-denial where He changes my practice before men. While I am already crucified positionally through the first, I must be crucified experientially on a continual basis through the second. Romans 6 conveys this dual reality: "Our old self *was* crucified with Him, . . . that we should no longer be slaves to sin; . . . Therefore do not let sin reign in your mortal body that you should obey its lusts" (verses 6, 12, NASB, emphasis added).

If we are going to minister effectively, we must be moving in the Spirit and not the flesh. If we are going to minister in the Spirit, the flesh must be continually crucified. If we are going to minister the truth of the cross to those under our care we must first understand it and practice it ourselves. You cannot lead people where you have not been. Finally, we must be able to articulate this vital discipline in terms people can understand.

Before I share what the Lord taught me about this process, I must sound a precaution. There are substitutes for dying to self. Included among them are:

- **Legalism**—Legalism aborts relationships with both God and others by its negative focus. The evil we seek to avoid grows—with concentration—into targets we cannot miss. Instead of limiting our sin, rules define sin, rivet our attention to it and lead us to desire it. In legalism, the flesh is in charge, taking the Holy Spirit's place, and thus is strengthened.
- **Religious Service**—It's easier to do good than be good. Watchman Nee observed,

  > If the flesh is not furnished opportunity to sin, it is willing to be involved in religious service where it is strengthened by exercise, thus providing Satan with an ongoing base of operations, until the opportunity to revert to sins occurs. And it surely will. If we don't forbid the flesh from doing good, we won't prevent it from doing evil. The best way to keep from sinning is to refuse to do any good in the flesh.

- **Emotional Experiences**—The flesh would rather sizzle than submit. It's possible to drown out conviction with the noise of assemblies. Great failures can follow great displays of emotion.
- **Correct Theology**—One can be correct in his or her understanding of doctrine and yet tolerate all the earmarks of unbroken self-will.
- **Counseling**—Receiving counseling can help us identify where and when the cross needs to be taken up. It pinpoints our Golgathas, but it doesn't

insure them. People often run from counselor to counselor seeking to avoid the cross.

- **Spiritual Warfare**—If this is not followed by cross-bearing, it will be less than effective. The absence of the cross gives place to the enemy (Ephesians 4:27).

- **Sorrows**—Faced with the inevitable sorrows of life, some say, "That's just the cross I'll have to bear." But sorrows are burdens we have to bear, and they are not synonymous with the cross. The issue is whether or not I will bear the cross in the midst of the burden, making it an occasion for growth and liberty. I have a choice—bitter or better? The application of the cross determines the outcome. That reality is summed up in the old adage that states: "The same sun that makes the butter soft makes the clay hard."

- **Time**—"Spiritual birthdays only tell us how long we've been on the road. They do not tell us how far we have traveled" (Vance Havner).

There are no substitutes for the cross! We must learn its dynamics and application. We said the cross was a place where a pattern was laid. In light of that, permit me to describe the elements of that pattern, based upon Jesus' cross experience. I will then attempt to relate them to our daily practice of the cross.

## The Calvary Pattern

1. *Jesus intentionally followed a distinct pattern*. Everything about His crucifixion followed an established

script. For example, in preparation for the Day of Atonement the high priest had to pronounce the atonement lamb as being acceptable and without blemish. So Jesus appeared before the high priest (Caiaphas) for that statement. When it did not come, He went to Pilate, who pronounced, "I find no fault in Him." This was according to the divine pattern, not coincidence.

The same could be said of the place, the timing and the method (cursed is everyone who hangs on a tree). Saints are not made in a night, and they are not made in their sleep! We must be aware of what is going on, as Jesus was. A.W. Tozer noted that a man on a cross didn't need anyone to tell him where he was. He knew. You will be able to recognize the cross when you are intentionally watching for it.

2. *Jesus laid down His life; no one took it from Him (John 10:17)*. Hebrews 7:27 tells us, "He offered up Himself" (NASB). John 19:30 informs us, "He bowed His head, and gave up His spirit" (NASB). John describes this event with the Greek word *paradidomi*. It refers to the voluntary submission of something that could not be taken by force. That means He died on a cross but not because of it. He did not die as a victim of what others did to Him. His death was an exercise of His will. He was in control. It was from the inside out, not outside in. It was the result of His will, not external pressures. It was His choice, not His executioner's. He could have sustained His life indefinitely or died earlier to avoid pain. He did neither, but waited until all was finished and then yielded up His spirit.

3. *Jesus submitted to the leading of the Holy Spirit for this process*. "Through the eternal Spirit [He] offered Himself

without blemish to God" (Hebrews 9:14, NASB). It must be the same for us. Romans 8:13 states, "For if you are living according to the flesh, you must die; but if by the Spirit you are putting to death the deeds of the body, you will live" (NASB).

The Spirit must be in charge of the process. We have to take up our cross, but it's His role to tell us where and when to put it down and get on it. He translates my positional co-crucifixion with Christ into my personal experience, administering that death wherever it is needed.

4. *Jesus didn't crucify Himself. God employed people in the process.* It would be impossible for a man to crucify himself. And the flesh will not crucify itself. God uses people, both inside and outside the church. That is why isolation doesn't produce holiness. You don't become holy by crawling into a hole. You need to rub shoulders with people who rub you the wrong way!

Most of these encounters will take place within the church, which has much in common with a rock-polishing drum. As that device is rotated, the stones inside it collide with one another. Between them is a liquid, abrasive polishing compound. Consequently, the collisions result in the removal of accrued sediment and the smoothing of rough edges. The result is beautiful, rounded stones revealing their true colors. In the church, it is the Spirit who polishes us by calling us to grace and quietness when wounded. He reminds us it is better to suffer a wrong than to commit one.

When, like Mabel Francis, we ask God to teach us how to die, we begin to see things differently. Relational problems become opportunities for liberation, for in the final analysis it isn't the actions of people that persistently hurt you as much as your reactions. You are set free to discover that to forgive is to set a captive free—and discover the captive was you!

5. *Jesus didn't pick the people God used*. The Father did. We sometimes want to learn humility but not at the hands of certain people we know. We say, "Lord teach me, but don't use *him*! I couldn't bear to watch him act so smug." But the person who rubs across the grain of our ego the most is the one we most need to love; we won't be crucifying the flesh until we do.

6. *Jesus accepted difficult circumstances*. Life is a school where we learn how to die so that we may learn how to live. Paul recognized that and viewed suffering in light of the cross (2 Corinthians 4:7-11). He learned that hardships don't create our realities; they only reveal them. What they often reveal is the tendency of the flesh to look for safety and satisfaction in circumstances. But Adam and Eve weren't safe in Eden, and Satan wasn't satisfied in heaven. In contrast, three Hebrew young men were both safe and satisfied in a furnace.

7. *Jesus didn't pick the time or place for His cross—the Father did*. Our part is to take up our cross; His part is to tell us when and where to put it up and get on it.

8. *Crucifixion is painful*. Dying to the flesh hurts because God is tearing the very fabric of our lives, uprooting practices and attitudes that have been securely in place for years, removing our emotional security blankets. Like Israel in the wilderness, longing for Egypt, we

long for the predictable and the familiar. This is why some folks "church hop." They are avoiding their cross.

9. *In crucifixion, Jesus was exposed and laid bare before the public*. To bear the cross is to confront ourselves as we are with Judgment Day honesty—and that's no easy task. One of the last lies we jettison is our idealized vision of ourselves. When God starts to confront us we may resort to denial, projecting our faults onto others or inappropriate spiritualizing, redefining our vice as virtue ("I'm not insulting and insensitive, I'm just too honest for my own good!").

It's one thing to say, "I'm sinful." It's quite another to get specific and confess, "I'm controlling, proud, insecure, etc." That only occurs when we allow God to expose us as we bear our cross.

10. *Crucifixion takes time*. It requires "a long obedience in the same direction" and the training of the senses through repetition. This is the process aspect of the sanctified life. Tozer said, "God will not bow to our nervous haste, . . . The man who would die to self must know that the way to become skillful is to do things over and over until he can do them perfectly."

11. *Jesus' crucifixion was public*. Some aspects of ours will be also. Great discretion is required in this, but when God orders public confession, it is an essential aspect of the crucified life.

When we practice daily cross-bearing, we discover six wonderful benefits. These are:

- Victory over the flesh (the only way it is accomplished);

- Victory over Satan (God chose self-sacrifice to win His greatest battle over His toughest opponent);
- Great joy (the greatest barrier to joy is self-centeredness and control);
- Being exalted by God ("Whoever humbles himself will be exalted . . .");
- Greater fruitfulness in ministry (brokenness precedes fruitfulness. Jesus' greatest fruitfulness was after the cross);
- A greater knowledge of God ("I want to know Christ . . . and the fellowship of sharing in his sufferings, becoming like him in his death" [Philippians 3:10]).

It takes a crucified man or woman to bear effective witness to a crucified Savior. We cannot bypass the cross on the way to effective ministry. One of our greatest needs is men and women who will minister the cross by carrying their own and inviting those they lead to "Follow, as I follow the Lord."

# The Cross of Jesus Christ and Revival

*by Fred A. Hartley III*

As we step into the twenty-first century, there is more and more talk about revival. At the same time, there is more and more misunderstanding about revival. Some think in terms of a laughing revival or a barking-like-a-dog revival or a quacking-like-a-duck revival. We need to be clear when we talk about revival, what we are talking about. We are not talking about an Assembly of God revival, a Vineyard revival, a Baptist revival or even an Alliance revival. We are talking about a *biblical* revival: the manifest presence of Christ.

Exhibit A of true revival is found in Acts 2. No one can argue with the fact that God's Holy Spirit was poured out in fullness upon that Upper Room gathering. Those 120 believers experienced an obvious and authentic move of the Holy Spirit. All the primary and secondary evidences of spiritual awakening mentioned by Dr. Richard Loveless in his book, *Dynamics of Spiritual Life*, are found right there in the first-century church. Upon closer investigation, we discover that at the heart of that first-century revival was the preaching of the cross of Christ by Peter. This classic sermon is studied in virtually every homiletics class around the world. It is regarded by many as a masterpiece. It follows the classic sermon outline of hook, book, look, took.

*Hook.* Peter uses the illustration of those who are speaking in tongues and declares, "These men are not drunk, as you suppose" (2:15). With those words he had them eating out of the palm of his hands.

*Book.* He takes them immediately to the prophet Joel and explains the work of the Holy Spirit. Then he moves from the Person of the Holy Spirit to the Person of the Lord Jesus Christ by quoting several messianic prophecies from the Book of Psalms.

*Look.* The preacher then takes a long hard look at the life of Jesus as it was lived out before their eyes and expounds on His superiority to King David, who was buried there in Jerusalem.

*Took.* The application occurs in the culmination of his speech: "Therefore let all Israel be assured of this: God has made this Jesus, whom you crucified, both Lord and Christ" (2:36). What we see vividly demonstrated in this Exhibit A account of true Holy Spirit revival is that it was preceded by fervent, united, corporate prevailing prayer, and it was triggered by preaching on the cross of Jesus Christ.

The response to Peter's sermon was phenomenal. We marvel that there were 3,000 Jews who were saved and baptized that day, but what was equally remarkable was not simply the breadth of the revival but the depth of it. We read, "When the people heard this, they were cut to the heart and said to Peter and the other apostles, 'Brothers, what shall we do?' " (2:37). The phrase "cut to the heart" is the same word used of the spear thrust in Jesus' side. The Greek word *katenugesan* means "they were stuck, pricked, punctured, cut wide open."

R.C.H. Lenski, in his classic commentary on the Book of Acts, says, "Like a sharp spear penetrated their hard and impervious hearts . . . in a deadly way . . . their entire previous attitude of unbelief was struck a deadly blow. These men felt utterly crushed." This is what is referred to among revivalists as "rock-bottom repentance." Notice that this response was triggered by the preaching of the death, burial and resurrection of Jesus Christ. It was a divine moment when God took the scales off the eyes of the unbelieving Jews and enabled them to see for the first time the grave consequences of their sin in the brutal execution of Messiah Jesus.

The question can logically be raised, "How can 3,000 unbelieving Jews wake up one morning as unbelievers and become fully devoted followers of Jesus Christ by noon?" The answer: it can easily happen once they see the reality of the cross of Jesus Christ.

Not only did the cross of Jesus Christ usher in this first Pentecostal revival, but the cross of Jesus Christ has also ushered in revival throughout church history. My own awareness of God's Spirit at work through revival was heightened by my joyful acquaintance over the years with Armin Gesswein. His first revival experience took place in his own local church on Long Island. Here is how he describes what happened:

> We, as Lutherans, always took Communion seriously. But this one Sunday was categorically different. Higher. More serious than ever before.

God convicted my heart over the sin within my congregation. People who came to church every Sunday had some of the worst reputations in town. They had been dishonest in their business dealings, prideful in their relationships and generally discrediting to the Gospel of Christ.

On Sunday, the Lord's Supper had been prepared. It sat conspicuously on the Communion table. Every worshiper who walked into our sanctuary could easily see it front and center. As I stood to preach I told the people with deep conviction and a trembling voice, "Today I have an unusually heavy heart. I am unable to serve us the Lord's Supper because of the obvious sin in our congregation. God would not be pleased with me as your pastor if I allowed any of us to receive Communion in our current condition. We are not ready to take the Lord's Supper. There is sin, even gross sin, in our church. God is a holy God and we must not come carelessly to His table. He said that we must be holy even as He is holy. He told us to examine His sacrifice and to examine ourselves. Just consider the cross of Christ. Consider the price Christ paid for us. How can we, an unholy people, put the bread and juice to our lips?

"I call us to repent now from sin, to renounce it and to get right with God today. Get your hearts right with God. Do whatever it takes. Then those who are ready will be allowed to receive from the Lord's Supper next Sunday."

You could have heard a pin drop. I knelt down in the front of my chair. Others knelt in their pews. There was silence. Even the organ sat quietly. Then there was weeping. People stayed there a long time. People prayed openly confessing sin, making restitution. People got right with people from whom they had been alienated for years. That week people paid overdue bills. They cleaned up their lives. God visited us that day at our church in a mighty way at the Communion table. I will never forget that moment as long as I live. And that church would never be the same. Our town was never the same.

In fact, when I walked from the church that day, the Holy Spirit stopped me on the sidewalk and said, "Armin, revival is your ministry." I have never wanted to settle for anything less than that since.

Categorically, this is the true biblical revival I am praying for. It is revival that comes from brokenness, humility, repentance, transparency and contrition. Revival purges, purifies, cleanses and restores. Revival brings integrity, morality and vitality. Revival begins at the cross of Jesus Christ and leads us on into the resurrection.

It is from the cross that all Christian virtues flow. In order for authentic revival to take place, there must be a rediscovery of the cross of Jesus Christ.

Recently I spoke seven times at a Christian college on the hot topic of revival. In this setting I often ask the students to complete this sentence, "Revival is . . ." It was glorious to hear their answers called out from all over the auditorium: Revival is . . . Jesus . . . freedom . . . God's manifest presence . . . repentance . . . deliverance . . . reconciliation between people . . . holiness . . . messy . . . tithing . . . love . . . heaven on earth . . . prayer . . . peace . . . glory . . . worship . . . joy.

As I listen to their responses during this exercise, I often see God painting a glorious mural of a preferable future that God desperately desires for us and that we desperately need. It is gripping. Compelling.

Then I ask the students to complete a second statement: "Revival results in . . ." The answers are equally invigorating: Revival results in . . . soul winning . . . moral purity . . . benevolence . . . social action . . . lives transformed . . . miracles . . . world missions . . . social justice . . . signs and wonders . . . the awe of God . . . public recognition that God is up to something . . . reconciled messages . . . parents loving children . . . children loving parents . . . conviction of sin both inside and outside the church . . . healing of personal dysfunction . . . healing of church dysfunction . . . healing of social dysfunction. You can feel the temperature in the room rising. Students begin clapping, cheering. It is electrifying. Then I direct the students into prayer clusters with three or four others and call out to God first for revival and then for the results of revival.

[One] night God made His holy presence known on campus, leading many students in deep repentance, brokenness and contrition. Many phoned their parents to bridge gaps of alienation. Some confessed sins to others and received prayers of forgiveness and deliverance. And some received Jesus Christ as Savior. Many were filled with the Holy Spirit. It was pure, cleansing, refreshing and revitalizing. And it all flowed out of the cross of Jesus Christ. It is the cross of Jesus Christ that brings purity to the work of revival in our humanity. It keeps the sinful nature in check and demons at abeyance.

Brokenness is, after all, the jewel of worship that is intended to drive the church. It comes in response to the cross of Jesus Christ. This brokenness is a result of a fresh revelation of the reality of Christ's atonement. The revelation of the holiness of God broke Isaiah wide open and led him to cry out, " 'Woe to me! . . . I am ruined! For I am a man of unclean lips, and I live among a people of unclean lips, and my eyes have seen the King, the LORD Almighty' " (Isaiah 6:5). Similarly God wants to lead us in such deep contrition in response to the fresh revelation of His holiness.

Isaiah went on to say regarding this brokenness, "For this is what the high and lofty One says—he who lives forever, whose name is holy: 'I live in a high and holy place, but also with him who is contrite and lowly in spirit, to revive the spirit of the lowly and to revive the heart of the contrite' " (57:15). Here we see the connection once again between brokenness and revival. God loves to breathe new life into broken, crucified, dead things.

David affirms that this brokenness is most pleasing to God: "The sacrifices of God are a broken spirit; a broken and contrite heart, O God, you will not despise" (Psalm 51:17). It is when we die to self that Christ breathes His fresh revival life into us and into our local churches. There is nothing that will bring about this level of brokenness more fully than the revelation of our sinfulness in light of the cross of Jesus Christ.

This is the final answer to the worship wars. I used to think that in order to really worship God, you needed to have a million-dollar pipe organ pounding out the hymns. Then as I got a little older I thought you needed to have guitars, drums, a praise band and worship team. Both perspectives missed the point. Now I have come to the conclusion that in order to truly worship God you need to have a broken and contrite heart.

Armin Gesswein referred to this pattern as "the law of revival," which he discovered while studying John 16:7-8: "But I tell you the truth: It is for your good that I am going away. Unless I go away, the Counselor will not come to you; but if I go, I will send him to you. When he comes, he will convict the world of guilt in regard to sin and righteousness and judgment."

Many of us have completely misunderstood this revival-prayer principle. We erroneously pray for the Holy Spirit to convict the world of sin and righteousness and judgment as if the Holy Spirit is going to fall on unbelievers and bring them under conviction. This completely misses the point. Armin accurately refocuses our attention on the sequence of Holy Spirit conviction. Notice the words, "I will send him to you. When he comes he will convict the world of guilt in regard to sin and righteousness and judgment." That is to say, God first sends His Holy Spirit to His people; then *through God's people* the Holy Spirit will bring conviction on the world. God will not violate this principle. Armin stated "God's Law of Revival" this way:

- The Holy Spirit brings conviction of sin to non-Christians to the measure in which He first brings conviction of sin on Christians.
- The unconverted feel their need of salvation when Christians first feel the need for them to be saved.
- When Christians feel their deep need for the Holy Spirit, non-Christians will feel their need for Christ.
- The church must be concerned for the world if the world is to be concerned for Christ.
- Non-Christians will deal with their sins according to the way Christians first deal with theirs.
- When Christians repent, sinners will repent.
- When revival is strong in the church, evangelism will be strong in the world.

This is the heart of Jesus' Upper Room teaching in John 16. This is the heart of the Upper Room experience in Acts 2. And it is the heart of authentic revival through history. The fresh revelation of the cross of Jesus Christ triggers both revival in the church and evangelism in the world. The purity of revival is guarded by the cross of Jesus Christ. As we pray toward true biblical revival and as we preach toward the full outpouring of God's Spirit on the church that we so desperately need, let's be sure to remain cross-focused so we don't get crossed up.

# The Cross of Jesus Christ and Education

*by David E. Schroeder*

H is name was nailed above Him on the cross: "This is Jesus, the King of the Jews." People scoffed at Him: "Come down from the cross, Messiah, and we will believe you." But only part of Him came down from the cross—His flowing blood.

His kingship they could mock; His messianic claim they could doubt. But even the most cynical of the crowd would readily call Him "Teacher." And that He was—*par excellence*. No man's mind could compete with His. His depth, His wit, His pedagogical versatility, His prophetic wisdom, His intentional obscurity at times and piercing clarity at others and, above all, His authority as a Teacher were unparalleled.

He was an intellectual and spiritual surgeon. In one statement He could perform incision, repair and suturing, such as when He said compassionately, "Neither do I condemn thee: go, and sin no more" (John 8:11, KJV). Or when He said sarcastically, "Which [one] of these . . . was [the] neighbor?" (Luke 10:36, KJV). Or "Render therefore unto Caesar the things which are Caesar's; and unto God the things that are God's" (Matthew 22:21, KJV).

Yes, His teaching was exceptional. Even from the cross He taught. And His words from the cross would ring down the corridors of time to provide an educational model for all His disciples. For example, consider His words, "My God, my God, why have you forsaken me?" (27:46). A credible education must take into account the existential dilemma faced by modern and postmodern thinkers—namely, our personal, social and spiritual alienation. Whether Jesus was truly forsaken or only thought He was, the sense of loneliness and estrangement was real for Him. His Gethsemane premonition of this moment terrified His soul because He knew the awful price of sin. Alienation for Jesus was not merely a psychological awareness of cosmic isolation; He knew that the soul being separated from its Source was, as Kierkegaard said, "The Dreadful that has already happened." He also knew that the eternal sequel to this alienation would be damnation.

In our natural mind, our uneducated state, humans don't get it. "There is no one who understands, no one who seeks God" (Romans 3:11). In condemnation, with sin still infesting our souls, we are abandoned by God. He always abandons sin. That's what it means to be holy, the essential attribute of His nature. An education that does not begin with a realistic instruction about the nature of mankind is inadequate, if not fraudulent.

At some point, He called out, "I am thirsty" (John 19:28). Not surprising, He was choking on the dust of death. Jesus suffered. The ultimate puzzle of metaphysical thinkers—if God is all good and all-powerful, why does He allow evil and suffering in the world? Irony of ironies, the One who gave living water that would make an immoral Samaritan woman never thirst again could not sate His own soul with even a drop of water. Instead, only a sponge full of vinegar was lifted to His dying lips. The symbolism is powerful. It was a bitter cup He was drinking, right up to the end. Job didn't get an answer and neither did Jesus. Instead, they got enough of God to swallow their question and move on with life or death. An honest education doesn't try to force answers where there are none, but it invites ongoing inquiry rather than cynicism. We continue to thirst for answers that will come only when we finally drink from the Fount. That's part of education—to teach humility in the face of intellectual finitude.

The thirsty, alienated Crucifix was not, however, self-absorbed. In His dying moments He continued the mission of His life—namely, the reconciling of humans with God. To all humans, even the despicable torturers who were taunting Him, He said, "Father, forgive them, for they do not know what they are doing" (Luke 23:34). By this statement, the Teacher gives the highest urgency to the work of reconciliation. Education that allows for lingering prejudices, petty partisanship and slanderous stereotyping is woefully incomplete. In fact, it is sinful, because it caters to inequity.

Children, even in their less-than-innocent state, know nothing of the prejudices that partition human groups by race, ethnicity, gender, religion, generation and social standing. They have to be indoctrinated into such thinking. And indoctrination is not education. From the cross God yells out to humanity, "I am paying a huge price to become friends with you and for you to become friends with each other. I do forgive you, even in your ignorance about crucifying the Messiah, but you must forgive each other if you expect Me to forgive you." "Reconciliation 101" needs to be on your transcript as a course you passed if you expect to graduate into God' presence.

An adequate education also teaches an accurate worldview. Jesus did it with one word: "paradise." To the penitent thief impaled on the cross next to His, Jesus said, "Today you will be with me in paradise" (Luke 23:43). While the thief likely did not receive this as a lecture in cosmology but as a word of great comfort, those who were listening learners heard a sure word about the reality that lies beyond the material world. No doubt the Sadducees and their ilk considered it to be delusional babbling, believing in neither the Scriptures nor the resurrection.

Educators today are being coerced to acknowledge that every worldview is a faith worldview. The logical positivists' claim that only those statements are meaningful that can be empirically verified have been impaled on their own spear because their own premise is then unverifiable. Their empirical, material worldview is predicated on a faith assumption just as surely as the statement, "In the beginning, God. . . ."

The worldview Jesus taught from His Roman lectern is a supernatural worldview; that is, a worldview that affirms or at least allows for realities that transcend the natural. Paradise, presumably the immediate presence of God, is the destination of the penitent.

This worldview presupposes an understanding of the human psyche. Jesus gave the most important and basic lesson in psychology when He uttered, "Father, into your hands I commit my spirit" (23:46). Unitary, dualistic and tripartite psychological schools can mount strong evidence in support of their positions, and this word from Jesus does not settle that debate. Freud's psychoanalysis, Skinner's behaviorism and modernists' Third Force perspectives can neither confirm nor debunk the simple statement of Jesus that part of being human is being spiritual. An education that ignores this fact reduces humanity to biology. That concept died with modernism, and postmoderns know Jesus was in touch with the nature of His real self when He commended His spirit into God's hands.

Speaking of postmoderns, they have got to love the relational concern of Jesus, even in His dying moment. "Dear woman, here is your son. . . . Here is your mother" (John 19:26-27). Education that is relationally illiterate has no future in our world. And as the graying of America continues with the "Boomer" generation just a decade away from retirement, intergenerational relationships will become increasingly important. The young have much to learn from the old, and the old may have even more to learn from the young as society becomes increasingly sophisticated technologically. Therefore, intergenerational compassion will be a hallmark of a truly Christian education. Self-serving as it may sound, one way the church can convince the watching world of the genuineness of its faith is to follow the Old Testament ideal of caring for the aging.

Furthermore, an education that ignores the linking of mother to son and father to daughter ignores a primal need that God has engineered for a healthy humanity. The depersonalizing of society, a byproduct of the technology age, can produce domestic isolation. Without any question, the key factor in adolescent rebellion is anger against parents, especially dads. Learning effective parenting skills may be one of the most important elements of an holistic education. Coming to the cross to hear Jesus emphasize this important bonding is a good place to start.

Finally, a comprehensive education speaks to the ultimate of historical moments. The sense of dramatic or redemptive history that Jesus demonstrated from the cross cannot be trumped. The most profound word, the word that divides history, that changed the human calendar, that echoes in the corridors of paradise is "finished" (19:30), Jesus' last word from the cross.

What was finished? His life? No, He knew and prophesied that He would resurrect. What He finished was the victory of God over evil, of redemption over damnation, of life over death. Salvation history's apex was that historical moment when history invaded eternity and brought it to earth. Millions of earthlings have become heavenlings since then. An education that doesn't know this lesson doesn't know what history is about. History without *His* story is merely time in chaos. But Jesus on the cross makes sense of it all.

All of us have much to learn from the Teacher as we stand, sit or bow in the classroom of the cross:

- A credible education must take into account our personal, social and spiritual alienation.
- An honest education doesn't try to force answers where there are none, but it invites ongoing inquiry rather than cynicism.
- The Teacher gives the highest urgency to the work of reconciliation.
- An adequate education also teaches an accurate worldview.
- Jesus gave the most important and basic lesson in psychology when he uttered, "Father, into your hands I commit my spirit" (luke 23:46).
- Education that is relationally illiterate has no future in our world.
- The most profound word, the word that divides history, that changed the human calendar, that echoes in the corridors of paradise, is "finished."

*The Practicality of the Cross*

# The Cross of Jesus Christ and the Christ Life

*by Gerald E. McGraw*

A country's flag is its symbol. It stands for that nation's monarch or president, its people, its reputation, its heritage.

What is the universal symbol of Christianity? The cross. When Christians mention "the cross," they are referring to Jesus' death in our place rather than to two huge ancient pieces of splintery wood nailed together. Paul wrote:

> For Christ did not send me to baptize, but to preach the gospel—not with words of human wisdom, lest the cross of Christ be emptied of its power.
>
> For the message of the cross is foolishness to those who are perishing, but to us who are being saved it is the power of God. (1 Corinthians 1:17-18)

This chapter relates Jesus' death to our ability to live the Christ life. Though Paul spoke wisely and baptized converts (Acts 16:31-33), his primary assignment focused on the saving gospel and on urging believers to live the Christ life.

From antiquity, a king or governor has had authority to pardon a convict. Often this occurs because evidence has surfaced demonstrating that person's innocence. Without Christ's cross, however, *we* have no innocence. We *are* guilty. No new evidence can prove we never sinned. Knowing the worst about us, Jesus willingly took our death and arose to justify us. Since He claimed authority to lay down His life and then to resume it (John 10:17-18), Jesus' resurrection completes the full message of the cross.

As I write these lines, my six-year-old grandson sits at my feet looking at the pictures in a Bible storybook. He just exclaimed, "There's Jesus! He had so much power that He came back alive!" Jesus did not remain dead. He proclaimed, "I am the Living One; I was dead, and behold I am alive for ever and ever!" (Revelation 1:18).

When I realize the need to trust Christ alone for salvation, I see "the Son of God, who loved me and gave himself for me" (Galatians 2:20)—the heart of the gospel. These next paragraphs will examine the *other* side of the gospel—how Jesus' death and resurrection provide us power today to *behave* like the holy Jesus.

We love Him for dying in our place. Do we also love Him so much that we are willing to surrender *everything* to Him? This involves experiencing His complete love, so that you love Him with your whole heart, soul, mind and strength. This also includes loving others: "But if anyone obeys his word, God's love is truly made complete in him. . . . If we love one another, God lives in us and his love is made complete in us" (1 John 2:5; 4:12).

As believers, have we sensed our slavery to selfish living so that we long for a remedy? Have we yearned for God's love to be made complete within us? Paul uses himself as an example of discovering the remedy: "I have been crucified with Christ and I no longer live, but Christ lives in me. The life I live in the body, I live by faith in the Son of God" (Galatians 2:20). So the cross has a vital relation to the Christ life.

In review, Galatians 2:20 shows us Jesus' love—that He chose to die in our place. Yet the same verse unveils the vital importance of learning *how* to live the Christ life, or, in other words, a Christ-filled life. This Scripture shows that when Jesus died, the Christian positionally and potentially died as well: "I have been crucified with Christ . . . but Christ lives in me."

Shortly before Jesus began His earthly ministry, a rugged prophet appeared. We call that bold, outspoken man "John the Baptist," not because he founded any Baptist church, but because he baptized many people. Yet John did not baptize just anyone. He required people to repent of their sins and find forgiveness by trusting the wonderful One who was soon to appear—Jesus.

John even baptized Jesus. Why did John do this when Jesus had never sinned? Jesus explained, " 'Let it be so now; it is proper for us to do this to fulfill all righteousness' " (Matthew 3:15). Those words are difficult to fully grasp. Although he jumps far beyond literal translation, Eugene Peterson properly catches the fact that Jesus' baptism is a gigantic, earthshaking event that portrays

Jesus' then-future cross and resurrection. Peterson's version reads: " 'Do it. God's work, putting things right all these centuries, is coming together right now in this baptism.' So John did it."

Obviously to us, Jesus' plunge into muddy Jordan predicts His death and burial to wash away sinners' sins. Arising from Jordan pictures Jesus' rising from the grave to declare sinners clean.

It is crucial that a new Christian (and long-time ones as well) grasp the simple lesson on how to succeed as God's child. I'm alive in Christ; now how do I live consistently? Can I overcome? What principles can supply the endurance to win the race? Romans 6 is probably the clearest Bible passage to help God's people find success in consistent living. Here we learn that Jesus who died to make us Christians also died so Christians can rise above wavering self-filled living. We are *in* the race. Now we must *win* the race.

Not only must I see that my old self potentially *died* with Jesus on the cross, but I now must make a new start by counting it true that when Jesus died, I died to the self-life. I remain out of the self-life's reach as I continually count myself dead to sin.

I also continue counting myself *alive* to God. Jesus rose so I can live an overcoming life by the Spirit's power. Careful study of God's remedy in a crucial doctrinal passage (below) provides vital help in understanding and taking the remedy:

> Or don't you know that all of us who were baptized into Christ Jesus were baptized into his

death? We were therefore buried with him through baptism into death in order that, just as Christ was raised from the dead through the glory of the Father, we too may live a new life. (Romans 6:3-4)

This victorious experience is preeminent in the Christ life. Without it, I am a seriously ill patient. Such a patient (1) must admit having a potentially fatal disease and (2) must know a well-proven remedy. (3) Yet if the patient never actually *takes* that remedy, serious peril continues. The patient must take the remedy.

I know, for example, of three individuals who recently failed to follow medical instructions and fell into desperate problems. In one case, our family was called to pray for a close relative in ailing health. God answered by reminding the patient of dietary steps to follow. She obeyed and prompt healing came.

Similarly, a Christian who has never entered the Christ life "lives dangerously." What is the cure for that "patient"?

1. *Grasp the serious need.* Self-life control involves a potentially fatal spiritual disease, a constant battle. "For the mind-set of the flesh is death, but the mind-set of the Spirit is life and peace. For the mind-set of the flesh is hostile to God because it does not submit itself to God's law" (8:6-7, HCSB).

2. *See the remedy.* "Our old self was crucified with him so that the body of sin might be done away with, that we should no longer be slaves to sin. . . . Count yourselves dead to sin but alive to God in Christ Jesus (6:6, 11).

Because Jesus died and arose to empower us, Christians need not be chained by a self-centered life. John the Baptist had earlier told his converts about the remedy:

"I baptize you with water for repentance. But after me will come one who is more powerful than I. . . . He will baptize you with the Holy Spirit and with fire . . . burning up the chaff with unquenchable fire." (Matthew 3:11-12)

Jesus would baptize these new believers with the "Holy Spirit and with fire." This phrase suggests an equipping provided by God's Spirit, who ministers both as fire to burn rubbish and wind to power victorious living. In the original New Testament language, the word "Spirit" is also the word "wind." "Wind" and "fire" portray inward purifying. Both are vivid biblical symbols of God's Spirit.

A dust rag or mop may chase away superficial dirt on a varnished surface or floor. Yet ground-in black marks on a floor covering may require vigorous use of scouring powder. Similarly, the human spirit needs a powerful purging. Robert Lowry wrote:

What can wash away my sin?
   Nothing but the blood of Jesus;
What can make me whole again?
   Nothing but the blood of Jesus.

As we have noted, John the Baptist proclaimed that Jesus "will baptize you with the Holy Spirit and with fire." Jesus connected the initial fulfillment of this powerful prediction with Pentecost when believers experienced purifying and empowering. After His resurrection, Jesus said, "For John baptized with water, but in a few days you will be baptized with the Holy Spirit" (Acts 1:5). It was not accidental that "When the day of Pentecost came, . . . suddenly a sound like the blowing of a violent wind came from heaven and filled the whole house. . . . All of them were filled with the Holy Spirit" (2:1-4). In the early church and today, God's Spirit wants to keep purifying and empowering believers.

When Jesus experienced water baptism, God's Spirit immediately came upon Him "in bodily form like a dove" (Luke 3:22). As we have seen, baptism illustrates the way to a victorious life.

The other Christian ordinance, the Lord's Supper, re-enacts time after time our dependence on the once-for-all cross to experience a continuing Christ-centered life. We constantly need the sanctifying spiritual food and drink represented by bread and juice. Christ's provision nourishes us spiritually.

In Holy Communion we should partake of Jesus' body for spiritual nourishment and His blood for spiritual purification. No magic can change bread into a body or juice into blood. Instead, when we partake of the bread with the hands and mouth, we should as well partake of the Bread of Life with our spirits by faith. We should not only drink the juice from a cup, but we should also trust Christ to keep on cleansing our spirits through His powerful, permanently effective blood. His blood alone can keep us holy.

In the Upper Room, shortly before Calvary, Jesus stressed five vital habits in living the Christ life:

- *Obey*. One cannot *earn* God's gifts by obedience. Yet obeying shows that we love Jesus. The Master said, "If you love me, you will obey what I command" (John 14:15).

A pioneer church of about fifty in Western Canada (pastored by Henry Blackaby) had followed God's call to sponsor three mission churches in the local area. Then a group of believers from 500 miles away asked Blackaby's small flock to sponsor them too. After seeking God's guidance about this "impossible" plea, his church sensed this as God's call and obeyed. In a remarkably short time, God provided a pastor and a salary for the far-away group. We, too, must obey God's directions. If He tells us "venture," "with God all things are possible" (Matthew 19:26). The Christ life is a life of obeying.

- *Abide*. Jesus showed His men the necessity of centering life in Himself. We must remain in Christ, stay in Him, live in Him. Jesus illustrated this vital part of the Christ life with the grape vine. "Remain in me, and I will remain in you. No branch can bear fruit by itself; it must remain in the vine" (John 15:4).
- *Produce*. The Christ life plan involves much fruit. "I chose you and appointed you to . . . bear fruit—fruit that will last" (15:16).
- *Joy*. The Christ life brings abounding love as the sold-out believer gives joy to the Master and He enriches us with love and joy. "Now remain in my love . . . so that my joy may be in you and that your joy may be complete" (15:9-11).

- *Glory*. This term is normally a rich, thrilling, splendid idea. Jesus' high priestly prayer overflows with "glory" words used no fewer than nine times (John 17). Though the Christ life centers in the cross, it leads us to unspeakably amazing future glory—glorification. The Christ life lets us overcome the world, the self-life and the devil. Yet, "God forbid that I should glory" (Galatians 6:14, KJV). "May I never boast except in the cross" (6:14).

The Christ life is the human life that uplifts Christ. In the Christ life, the evil world has become an old, dead thing. Moreover, in entering and maintaining the Christ life, we choose to keep counting ourselves dead to sin but alive to God.

# The Daily Cross of Jesus Christ

*by Lisa M. Rohrick*

I had to get a new license plate on my car last year. Why? Because it was mandatory for every vehicle in the country of Benin, West Africa. It was a frustrating experience from beginning to end, including six visits to the Benin Department of Transport office (from now on referred to as BenDOT), countless hours standing in lines, two visits to an unmarked lot behind a cement factory to have the serial number checked, the paying of fees for every little piece of paper along the way and three visits to BenDOT's "Mission Control" yard.

Several weeks later I finally had a new license plate. It had been mounted crooked, but at least it was on the car. However, they had misspelled my name on my car papers, so the process still was not over. I made another five visits to the BenDOT office, each of them an average of three hours and with few results. My frustration and anger began to increase exponentially.

There is a Beninese proverb that says, "A fallen tree no longer suffers in the wind." In other words, that which is dead is no longer troubled by life's circumstances. God was using BenDOT to show me that the old me was still very much alive and suffering in the wind of African red tape.

## Don't Forget the Cross

Most of us will readily agree that we are saved by Jesus' death on the cross. We affirm that the cross is central to Christianity, to our salvation. But do we forget the cross in our Christian lives? Do we behave as if we can leave that painful symbol behind us after having been there once? Do we simply want to enjoy being new creatures by the blood of Christ and seeking only the blessings that await us?

Jesus said, "If anyone would come after me, he must deny himself and take up his cross daily and follow me" (Luke 9:23). The word "daily" tells me that whatever this verse teaches is not reserved just for the day of our salvation, followed by occasional reminders at Good Friday services and participation in the Lord's Supper. It's something that must keep happening every day of our lives.

The image of carrying the cross comes from the Roman practice whereby the convicted criminal carried his own cross to the place of his crucifixion. Once that wooden crossbeam was placed on his shoulders, he knew his destiny. Humiliated and stripped of all liberties, he did only what he was ordered to do—trudge along the dreaded path to his death. He knew that suffering awaited him—intense suffering. He knew that he would not return. His life was over.

When Jesus invites us to take up our cross and follow Him, He invites us to march toward our death. He invites us to "Put to death, therefore, whatever belongs to your earthly nature: sexual immorality, impurity, lust, evil desires and greed" (Colossians 3:5). It is by the cross that we are sanctified, having "crucified the sinful nature with its passions and desires" (Galatians 5:24).

But the reality is that it hurts to die. It hurts to have my pride torn from my heart. It hurts to kill my dreams and fantasies, having their roots ripped from the center of my being. Sometimes I don't want to crucify the passions and desires of my old nature.

Notice that Jesus introduces His invitation with the words, "If anyone would. . . " (Luke 9:23). He leaves the choice with us. Will we deny ourselves and carry our cross? The invitation is not very appealing. Who wants to be humiliated and stripped of all liberties? Who wants to hand over his rights? Who wants to be a "living sacrifice" (Romans 12:1)? Who wants to die—every day?

The person who wants to die is usually the one who is tired of living a life of failure. It's the university graduate doing the only job he could find—washing dishes in a restaurant. It's the patient in the rehabilitation hospital whose whole being screams out in protest to the captivity of a wheelchair. It's the missionary who is annoyed with all the red tape and is ashamed at her inability to control her temper. It's the Christian who has tried to live independently of the cross, rejecting its shame, but in the end realizing that there is no other route than to follow the Master who, "for the joy set before him endured the cross, scorning its shame" (Hebrews 12:2).

It may not be very inviting, but the only route to a life of victory—that of a true disciple—passes by the cross. And as we die, the cross changes from a symbol of death to a symbol of life as we catch a glimpse of new life on the other side—life in Christ. "For you died, and your life is now hidden with Christ in God" (Colossians 3:3).

As A.W. Tozer explained,

> The cross is rough and it is deadly, but it is effective. It does not keep its victim hanging there forever. There comes a moment when its work is finished and the suffering victim dies. After that is resurrection glory and power, and the pain is forgotten.

It is hard to die to self. But while I dread the pain and humiliation of my own crucifixion, I know it's the road by which I must pass. I long to "know Christ . . . and the fellowship of sharing in his sufferings, becoming like him in his death" (Philippians 3:10). And if I share with Him in His sufferings, I will also share with Him in His glory (Romans 8:17).

## A Personal Cross

Returning to Luke 9:23, notice that Jesus said if someone chooses to be a disciple, "he must deny himself and take up *his* cross daily and follow me" (emphasis added). Jesus did not call us to take up a rough Roman cross and carry it to Calvary where nails will be driven through our hands and feet. He already did that for us, dying in our place. That work is finished (John 19:30), done "once for all" (Hebrews 10:10).

But each of us has a personal cross to carry. It is a cross designed by our Father with our best interests in mind in order that we will be conformed to the image of His Son (see Romans 8:28-29). The Savior knows what is needed in each of His children to bring them to the point of death to self.

My friend, Caroline, has a serious kidney disease and spends five hours three days a week attached to a dialysis machine that filters toxins out of her blood. Dialysis wipes out her energy, and she is able to do very little else on those days. Caroline used to be very active, enjoying golf and other sports. She no longer has the strength for much physical activity. A number of years ago she received a kidney transplant. Hope sprang up within her that she would return to a normal life. Sadly, her body rejected the donor kidney, sentencing her to remain dependent upon the dialysis machine. She must follow a strict diet and has had several medical emergencies where her life hung in a balance.

Caroline's cross is a heavy one, but she has chosen to carry it with joy. She has difficult days when she would love to throw down her cross and run the other direction. But as the old Caroline dies on the cross of kidney disease, the new Caroline—"hidden with Christ in God" (Colossians 3:3)—shines through. Hours of forced inactivity have drawn her into study of God's Word by which she is being conformed into the image of the Lord Jesus Christ.

From time to time I have dropped by to visit Caroline. As we have talked and laughed and prayed together, I am the one who has come away encouraged. She is a vibrant example of the daily work of the cross of Jesus Christ in one of His children.

## The Cross of Persecution

For some of us, carrying the cross will mean persecution and rejection: a coworker who pokes fun at us because we don't laugh at his off-color jokes; sudden unemployment because we won't tell the lie our boss has directed us to tell; a spouse who leaves because he/she does not love the Lord.

When we preach the cross—which we must do since a crossless gospel is powerless and incomplete—we may feel the heat. The Apostle Paul suffered intensely for his bold proclamation of the message of the cross (see the summary of his experiences in 2 Corinthians 11:24-27).

Christian history is filled with stories of martyrdom—people who carried the daily cross of persecution to their death. These stories are not limited to the dusty tomes of church history. Martyrdom continues. Around the world, many thousands of Christians suffer and die because they simply refuse to renounce the name of Jesus Christ. The Church in the West has been largely sheltered from these horrors. But that may change. Persecution may be on its way. If the Western Church is given that cross, will we choose to carry it?

## Protected by the Cross

Today is a national holiday in Benin—Voodoo Day. Here in the birthplace of this demonic religion, hundreds of thousands of people live lives of fear, trying to appease evil spirits. Today they will slaughter sheep and goats and offer them to the enemy of their souls.

As I write, I am trying to block out the sound of incessant drumming. It's very different from the traditional Beninese rhythms I have grown to enjoy at church. This is the frenzied thumping of a voodoo ceremony—and it's coming from my next door neighbor's yard.

I took a break from my work to pray, claiming the protection of the blood of Christ over my life and my home. I do not need to fear the evil that surrounds me, because the Lord Jesus Christ has "disarmed the powers and authorities, [and] he made a public spectacle of them, triumphing over them by the cross" (Colossians 2:15). I can face evil unafraid because of the cross.

And so can all believers. We all may not have evil screaming at us from our neighbor's front yard, but the subtle wiles of Satan are no less evil than the blatant ones. Jesus died "to rescue us from the present evil age" (Galatians 1:4). We have an enemy, the devil, who "prowls around like a roaring lion looking for someone to devour" (1 Peter 5:8). But we can resist him. Whether it's the lure of the love of money, the deceptive philosophies of New Age teaching, pornography on the Internet or the false accusations of a coworker, the cross of the Lord Jesus Christ rescues us from it all. Daily.

## Keep It Central

The cross must remain central in every aspect of our lives—every day. In his book, *On a Hill Too Far Away*, John Fischer tells of a church in Old Greenwich, Connecticut with a ten-foot, rough wooden cross at the front of the sanctuary. This cross is not hanging decoratively behind the pulpit. It stands in the center of the sanctuary—between the pulpit and the pews. No matter what takes place in that sanctuary, the cross is in the way. The congregation must look around it to see the pastor preaching. Young actors in the children's Christmas play must work their way around the cross. It comes between the bride and groom in a wedding ceremony.

The placement of the cross in that church is uncomfortable. It gets in the way of everything. And that's the way it should be.

The cross must interfere in my life. I dare not allow it to be reduced to a pendant around my neck or fine artwork in the sanctuary of my church. Daily I must go to Jesus for the cleansing of His blood, presenting myself to Him as a living sacrifice, clinging to Him for new life and victory over sin. Daily I can trust in the cross, "the power of God" (1 Corinthians 1:18) to protect me from the evil of this age and to enable me to withstand attacks of the enemy. Daily I must carry the cross that Christ has given me to bear. For each of us the circumstances will be different, but the bottom line is the same: death to self and life in Christ.

Hallelujah for the cross!

*The Fourfold Gospel and the Cross*

# The Cross of Jesus Christ and Salvation

*by Robert B. Goldenberg*

M ost often when we look at the cross in our Christian lives, it is in the context of sanctification; that is, the willful act of dying to one's self. So how do we interact with the cross in the matter of salvation? To begin our discussion, let us consider two portions of Scripture. The first is First Corinthians 1:20-25:

> Where is the wise man? Where is the scholar? Where is the philosopher of this age? Has not God made foolish the wisdom of the world? For since in the wisdom of God the world through its wisdom did not know him, God was pleased through the foolishness of what was preached to save those who believe. Jews demand miraculous signs and Greeks look for wisdom, but we preach Christ crucified: a stumbling block to Jews and foolishness to Gentiles, but to those whom God has called, both Jews and Greeks, Christ the power of God

and the wisdom of God. For the foolishness of God is wiser than man's wisdom, and the weakness of God is stronger than man's strength.

Paul begins this section by asking four questions. The first three are calling for the best in human wisdom. "Where is the wise man? Where is the scholar? Where is the philosopher of this age?" In other words, where is the best that the human race has to offer? Then he points to a forgone conclusion: our very best, our wisest, our smartest and most profound have been turned to foolishness. Why? Because our best and wisest did not recognize God. What's more, God used foolishness to bring salvation. And that foolishness, simply put, was Christ crucified on the cross.

The second passage to consider is Romans 9:30-33:

What then shall we say? That the Gentiles, who did not pursue righteousness, have obtained it, a righteousness that is by faith; but Israel, who pursued a law of righteousness, has not attained it. Why not? Because they pursued it not by faith but as if it were by works. They stumbled over the "stumbling stone." As it is written:

"See, I lay in Zion a stone that causes
        men to stumble
    and a rock that makes them fall,
    and the one who trusts in him will
        never be put to shame."

In these verses we read that the Gentiles found righteousness by faith. At the same time Israel, while pursing righteousness, did not find it. Why? There are two reasons. First, they were trying to attain it by works of the law; second, they stumbled over the "stumbling stone." What is this "stumbling stone"? As we pursue this study, we will discover that it is again the cross.

## The Drive of Fallen Man

From the time Adam and Eve first sinned in the garden, man has had a drive to be in control. God gave them permission to eat from any tree in the Garden of Eden but one; man said let me at that one. This desire for control affects every area of life—even the search for salvation.

For example, we demand that the plan of salvation makes sense to us. The problem with this is clearly pointed out in Proverbs 16:25: "There is a way that seems right to a man, but in the end it leads to death." If humans had a part in designing the plan of salvation, we would bring together our best scholars, our best philosophers, our wisest men to come up with something that made sense to our finite minds. But our natural understanding is flawed and will lead to death. That, however, has not stopped man from designing his own plan of salvation.

In our desire to control we also want to make the rules. The basis for every cult and false religion is man's designer rules of salvation. We want to judge the efforts, weigh the labor and decide if our plan is being worked correctly. This runs into problems because we are limited in what we can see and understand. Jeremiah 17:9 tells us, "The heart is deceitful above all things and beyond cure. Who can understand it?" So how can we pass judgment on individual effort if we cannot even judge our own hearts?

Finally, man in all his wisdom wants to pronounce the saved. Since in our own thinking we are in control, in the end we say who goes to heaven and who does not. But Jesus specifically tells us in Luke 12:4-5 that man cannot determine this—only God can.

Unredeemed man sees all these forms of control as the answer. This way of thinking represents the work of our "best"—our wisest, our scholars, our philosophers. It is as if we have built a great ocean sailing ship. All our efforts have been brought together and poured into it. The mast is wonderfully carved. The sails are unfurled and caught up in the breeze. The flags are flying. The ship is beautiful. It is, after all, our best efforts.

Now, picture this ship sitting just outside the entrance to a harbor. The harbor is the final destination. It is heaven. But in between the ship and the harbor is a reef. There is no way past it. It blocks the harbor, and man in all his wisdom can't get beyond it.

## The Gift of a Gracious God

Man on his own can never achieve peace with God. God is holy. Man, however, is sinful. John tells us, "If we claim to be without sin, we deceive ourselves and the truth is not in us" (1 John 1:8). Here is where the cross enters the picture. With the cross God demonstrated His wonderful love for us. He sent His Son to die so that we could find life. With the cross God provided payment for our sin. "The wages of sin is death" (Romans 6:23), and Jesus paid the wage.

God made the rules simple: "Everyone who calls on the name of the Lord will be saved" (Acts 2:21). Man cannot work to attain this. He cannot earn it in any way. Salvation is a gift (see Ephesians 2:8-9). All of man's wisdom is meaningless in God's equation. And as for pronouncing the saved, according to Ephesians 1:4, that was done by God "before the creation of the world." Man's wisdom is left completely out of the picture.

## The Paradox

Remember the ship trying to get into the harbor? That ship, in all of its magnificent beauty, represents the best of man. Using all of our wisdom and understanding, we have built this superb vessel to get us into the harbor, but that reef is still blocking the way. The reef is God's plan. It is the cross and we cannot get around it. We look at it and call it foolishness. It is outside of our control and beyond our appreciation. What we call wisdom God calls foolishness.

We ask God for a sign—something we can get a handle on, something we can see and grasp. But He won't give us a sign; instead, He calls us to *trust* Him.

We offer Him our works—something we can do to convince God we are worthy. But He calls our best works filthy rags (Isaiah 64:6) and instead offers us *grace*.

We make an effort to obey the law, God's written standard of conduct. *At last, something tangible*, we think. The only problem is that no matter how hard we try, we cannot fully obey; we fall short every time. God tells us to let go of the law and grab hold of *faith*.

Trust, grace, faith—they are all so fuzzy, so hard to come to terms with. We want to guide our ship into the safety of the harbor—but we want to do so on our own terms. The cross blocks the way.

## The Open Door to Peace

And then God steps onto the distant shore. He calls to us: "Crash your ship on the reef! Go full speed ahead right into the cross!" We can't believe what we are hearing. That will destroy all our hard work. Our wisdom, our control, our rules will all be shattered. And that is exactly what must happen. On the wrong side of the cross it is viewed as a stumbling block. It looms up, jamming our way. Our wisdom cannot get past it. Our scholars are mystified by its simple message. Our philosophers are perplexed by its one-sided, grace-giving power. Grace is beyond their grasp. So they reject the cross and cry, "Build better ships. We'll find a way past it." But still it stands, keeping us out of the harbor unless and until we abandon all human effort and willingly collide with it.

It is in that collision that the cross changes from a barrier reef to a bridge. As our great ship is destroyed and we are helplessly thrown into the sea, we find that trusting God's understanding of salvation leads to hope. God's rules do work. The cross, which was so awkward and problematic, now becomes a treasure of dearest value. It goes from blocking our way to opening the way. It was not pushing us back out to sea; it was forcing us to abandon our wisdom for God's foolishness only to find that "the foolishness of God is wiser than man's wisdom, and the weakness of God is stronger than man's strength" (1 Corinthians 1:25).

# The Cross of Jesus Christ and Sanctification

*by Douglas B. Wicks*

"There is something in the cross which throughout all the ages is an abiding power in the sanctification of Christ's people."

—A.B. Simpson

Why is it that the short, uncomplicated imperatives in the Bible are often the most difficult to obey? "Love one another," "Pray continually," "Be holy" and "Follow Me" are just a few that come to mind. Who among us has obeyed these commands to the fullest? Yet no one would argue if we were to comply entirely with these imperatives, the quality of our spiritual lives would be much richer and more influential. Dietrich Bonhoeffer said, "One act of obedience is better than a hundred sermons."

Another brief verse that contains an apparent hard-to-follow imperative is First Peter 3:15: "In your hearts set apart Christ as Lord." These nine syllables are often glanced over both in our reading and in our practice. This is confirmed in the findings of Christian researcher George Barna: "Believers are largely indistinguishable from nonbelievers in the way they think and live."

It is becoming embarrassingly clear that something just doesn't match up to what many believers profess. Our talk doesn't manifest itself in our walk. And it is at this junction of our talk and our walk that the depth of our sanctification is revealed.

Let's take a closer look at the elements of this brief but important verse to see what we can learn about the relationship between the meaning of the cross and the doctrine of sanctification.

## "In Your Hearts" (The Will)

Dr. A.B. Simpson wrote, "The hardest thing to see and to crucify is our own self-confidence and self-will. We have to pass through many a painful incident and many a humiliating failure before we find it out and fully recognize it." This same thought is echoed in the book *Empowered!*, by professor Gerald McGraw: "The surrender of the will is the supreme surrender."

I will never forget an impressionable scene in the book *The Horse Whisperer*, a story about a cowboy who has the gift of breaking the wills of wild horses. The scene I remember is the defining moment in the story where the cowboy, with consummate patience, sits quietly in a pasture, waiting, waiting and waiting for the horse to turn and submissively come back to where the cowboy was sitting. What a picture of our merciful, loving God waiting for us to fully surrender our wills to Him.

As much as we might not like to admit it, the process of breaking the self-will—even of believers—is much like the difficult task of breaking the will of a wild horse. In *The Self-Life and the Christ Life*, Simpson wrote: "The very first thing you need in order to be of any use anywhere is to be thoroughly broken, completely subjected and utterly crucified in the very core and center of your will."

One of the fond memories of my youth is going with my dad on Sunday evenings to Park St. Church in Boston to hear the preaching of Dr. Harold J. Ockenga. On one such occasion he pronounced, "The reason so few people are filled with the Spirit is that so few completely turn over to Him control of every realm." As a young boy I could not have known the depth of that truth, but now as a grown man I see it as one of the keys to living a powerful and victorious Christian life.

If the issue of the battle of the will is not dealt with early in our Christian lives, we will not only squelch our spiritual growth, we will waste precious time fighting the civil war within us. G. Campbell Morgan said, "Abandonment to God is not merely the act of enlisting as soldiers to fight battles—that is a secondary matter; it is first the abandonment of self to the Spirit of God, that He may purify and cleanse from everything that is unlike His own perfection of beauty."

Yielding our wills to Christ, dying to self, is particularly difficult for North Americans to achieve. We are ingrained from childhood to be self-made, strong-willed, self-confident and in control. The concepts of surrender, obedience and humility are hardly virtuous characteristics to pursue. This sociocultural influence feeds our "old nature" with which we are all infected at birth. But just as the curtain in the temple was torn in half when Christ died on the cross (Matthew 27:51), so, too, at the death of our self-life, the threads of self in our old nature will be severed, enabling us to don the clothes of a new nature.

The starting point of living a sanctified life, then, is becoming dead to self and alive unto Christ. Simpson said, "It is not until self dies that Christ can be enthroned as King in our hearts and lives." More recently, Dr. John Harvey wrote in an *Alliance Life* article, "One needs to come to an end of self, in brokenness and emptiness, so that he can be resurrected to a walk with God."

## "Set Apart" (Sanctify)

The phrase "set apart" in this verse means to sanctify or to make holy. This is the imperative we are to obey. There is no equivocation in the author's meaning. Oswald Chambers said, "The destined end of man is not happiness, nor health, but holiness. God's one aim is the production of saints."

It is important to note here that this phrase (i.e., "set apart") taken in context includes the prerequisite of dying to self. Only if we do that can we be empowered by the life of Christ within us. Alliance professor and author Dr. George Pardington said, "In sanctification we pass out of the self-life into the Christ-life."

The doctrine of sanctification is one of the distinctive emphases of The Christian and Missionary Alliance. It is represented as the laver in the C&MA logo. The laver symbolizes a "daily cleansing from sin and power for service through the indwelling Christ." Yet sanctification is so much more than a symbol or a wonderful theological truth. From the moment we receive Jesus Christ as our personal Savior, we are instantly justified and sanctified before God our Maker and heavenly Father, based on the redemption provided for us by the death of Jesus Christ on the cross.

Sanctification is a renouncement of all that a person desires. When someone asked George Mueller his secret for begin such a fruitful Christian, he replied, "There came a day when George Mueller died, utterly died! No longer did his own desires, preferences, and tastes come first. He knew that from then on Christ must be all in all!"

Practically speaking, sanctification is a renunciation of who we are, welcoming God's way instead of our own. Amy Carmichael expressed this beautifully in one of her devotional writings:

> Think through me, thoughts of God,
> My Father, quiet me,
> Till in Thy holy presence, hushed,
> I think Thy thoughts with Thee.

Imagine the sweetness of fellowship we will have with Christ if we become so lost in Him that the thoughts we think are His very own.

This is, of course, the essence of the teaching about the Christ life. Simpson said the Christ life

> is living the very life of another. It is to have the
> very person of Christ possessing our being—
> the thoughts of Christ, the desires of Christ,

the will of Christ, the faith of Christ, the purity of Christ, the love of Christ, the unselfishness of Christ, the single aim of Christ, the obedience of Christ, the humility of Christ, the submission of Christ, the meekness of Christ, the patience of Christ, the gentleness of Christ, the zeal of Christ—and the works of Christ manifest in our mortal flesh.

## "Christ as Lord" (Who's in Charge?)

The third element of our verse is indelibly linked to the first—the will. "Christ as Lord" refers to the kingship of Jesus in our lives. Most of us are grateful for His role as Savior, but we have a more difficult time *willingly* removing ourselves from the throne, allowing Jesus to take His rightful position as King. It is as unnatural for us to yield control to another as it was difficult for the hobbit, Bilbo, to hand over the powerful ring to Gandalf in J.R.R. Tolkien's series, *The Lord of the Rings*.

Can we describe ourselves as being willingly possessed by God? To be able to do so is a wonderfully pleasing and peaceful state. It is a condition understood by fewer and fewer Christians, although desired by so many. It is akin to what Tozer wrote about in *The Pursuit of God*. In his chapter entitled "The Blessedness of Possessing Nothing," he wrote, "My heart [shall] have no need of the sun to shine in it, for Thyself wilt be the light of it, and there shall be no night there."

Our consumer-driven society knows little of this concept. It is natural for people to be turf protectors, to stubbornly refuse to give in. It is as though we claim squatter's rights on property that does not legally belong to us. And, the fact is, it doesn't! We are the creatures, fashioned by a powerful, loving God. Psalm 139:13-14 says, "You created my inmost being; you knit me together in my mother's womb. I praise you because I am fearfully and wonderfully made; your works are wonderful."

Would we not think it shameful and contemptible for a child upon his twenty-first birthday to announce to his parents that he was throwing them out of their house? How heartrending to see them pack their belongings and walk dejectedly out the front door. In essence that is what we are doing to our Lord, who will not forcefully seize His rightful position in our lives.

## Cross Embracers

Jesus said, "If anyone would come after me, he must deny himself and take up his cross daily and follow me" (Luke 9:23). To take up one's cross involves a whole-hearted commitment. Did you ever try to hug someone with something in your hands? It never works. I like to give my wife a real hug when I leave for work in the morning. I want her to feel hugged all day until I get home that evening. You can't hug effectively with one arm. It takes two. Total commitment.

That's what God wants us to do with the cross. He wants us to drop whatever we have in our hands, whatever we have in our hearts, that is getting in the way of a full-bodied embrace of the cross. I love the words of the song Steve Green sings about this:

Embrace the cross
Where Jesus suffered
Though it will cost
All you claim as yours.

Partial commitment is no commitment at all. And partial sanctification is to experience less than the abundant life that Jesus promised to those who believe. The Apostle Paul prayed, "May God himself . . . sanctify you through and through. May your whole spirit, soul and body be kept blameless at the coming of our Lord Jesus Christ" (1 Thessalonians 5:23). It is instructive to note that he was addressing Christians, not unbelievers.

Say no to self. Say yes to Christ. Live victoriously and abundantly. "In your hearts set apart Christ as Lord" (1 Peter 3:15).

# The Cross of Jesus Christ and Healing

*by John A. Harvey*

The biggest challenge of faith in trusting God for physical healing is not if God can, but if He will. It's not God's power that people doubt as much as God's "want to." Though the promises of God remain yea and amen, there is that feeling that God vacillates back and forth when deciding the cases He will heal.

God's unchanging character of compassion should be sufficient to remove our doubts, but the great majority of those who are *not* healed seems to provide evidence to the contrary. In The Christian and Missionary Alliance we provide more fuel for faith by affirming that healing is paid for in the atonement of Jesus Christ; therefore, we should expect God to want to heal us in the same way He wants to forgive us. The texts for this thinking come from Isaiah 53:4-5, where the prophet says, "He took up our infirmities" and "by his wounds we are healed." The parallel passage of Matthew 8:17 lets us know that the verses apply to physical needs and not only to our sin problem. In spite of these assurances, when people are not healed, it is God's "willingness" that is usually made the scapegoat.

However, the Scriptures make clear that the reasons why people are not healed most often rest with man and not God. The most common reason is our unbelief. A second reason, and the one to which this article is ad- dressed, is our failure to recognize the spiritual side of our physical problems. Our bodies are in sync with our soul and spirit, and problems in one area inevitably im- pact the other areas of our being. The causes of the body's sicknesses are often found to be in the spiritual part of man's being, and, therefore, the cure needs to also address the inner man as well as the outer man.

It is my understanding that the cross work of Christ is primarily addressing our physical infirmities by solving the spiritual causes for our afflictions. The application of the cross to illness is probably greater than the limited scope being considered in this article, but if the believer can understand the causes of his problems (i.e., get an ac- curate diagnosis of the disease), then faith can flourish from insight and healing will be forthcoming.

## The Curse

The Scriptures let us know that the causes of illness find their source in (1) the curse, (2) acts of sin and (3) the activity of the devil. While it might seem simplistic to lump all physical afflictions into one of the three catego- ries, it will be beneficial for this discussion to do so, and I believe the reader will conclude that this threefold ap- proach covers most situations.

The first of these causes refers to the curse God brought on creation due to the fall and is symbolized by the thorns and thistles that resulted and by the pain of childbirth. While it might sound foreign to our ears, the curse lets us know that God is Himself the cause of some diseases and ailments. In the Bible, God is the One who first utters curses. In the Law, God provides curses as well as blessings—and the curses include sickness (Leviticus 26:16). Many are the examples when Israel experienced the fulfillment of the curses, not the least of which are the plagues that came upon them in the wilderness.

At the waters of Marah (Exodus 15:22-27) God was teaching the people about sicknesses that came from His own hand when He said, " 'If you listen carefully to the voice of the LORD your God and do what is right in his eyes, if you pay attention to his commands and keep all his decrees, *I will not bring on you any of the diseases I brought on the Egyptians*, for I am the LORD, who heals you' " (15:26, emphasis added). The Egyptians had been under God's curse and were plagued as a result.

The context of the promise was the story of turning the poisonous waters of Marah into drinkable water by throwing in a piece of wood or a tree, which A.B. Simpson correctly recognizes as a type of the cross of Jesus (as portrayed in his hymn, "The Branch of Healing"). The bitter waters are like the curse that the cross transforms into blessing. In the same way the creation is under the curse that results in sicknesses of many kinds, but those who come to the cross have the curse changed to blessing so that God is not bringing on us any of the diseases He brought on the Egyptians.

Because Jesus became a curse for us on the cross (Galatians 3:13), He removes us from the position of the cursed to the status of being blessed. This change of status provides a protective covering for the redeemed from sickness in most instances and also a rationale for healing if God allows disease to hurt us. Faith in the cross work of Jesus trusts God to break the effects of the curse just as Moses healed the bitter waters with a piece of wood.

I recall one believer who rejected a medical diagnosis of cancer on the basis of being freed from the curse and continued to live a healthy life thereafter. No doubt it is one of those instances where "[as your] faith, [so] be it unto you" (Matthew 9:29, KJV). This much is biblically certain: the redeemed have changed status from being cursed to being blessed as a result of the cross of Jesus. The benefits of that transfer are limited only by our faith.

## Acts of Sin

A second cause of sickness is the sins we commit. When we think of sins causing illness, it is usually with the same rationale of Job's comforters: God judges people with physical affliction as a result of sins they have committed. The potential of judgment by God with sickness has already been alluded to under the discussion of the curse. In such instances God remains the source of the sickness. Conversely, I want to direct the reader to understand that sin of itself is a direct source of illness; sin causes our diseases.

It is a well-known medical fact that many of our bodily malfunctions are self-inflicted. Western society is afflicted with scores of ailments due to our overeating and decadent lifestyles. Greed, gluttony, envy, anger and fear work their effect on our bodies with ulcers, allergies, cancers and a host of other diseases all catalogued in Dr. McMillen's classic, *None of These Diseases*. Dr. Richard Swenson, in his books *Margin* (1982) and *The Overload Syndrome* (1993), convincingly describes the connection between our warped and stressed-out lifestyles with the diseases of our age. The conclusion is clear: our sins cause many of our diseases.

Healing from self-inflicted sicknesses must include the forsaking of the sins that caused the affliction. However, sin is a form of bondage, and we often lack the power to forsake our sins. Sin is also defiling, so that in addition to forsaking one's sins, a person needs to be cleansed as well. It is the shed blood of Jesus on the cross that forgives, cleanses and delivers from sin (1 John 1:7-2:2). It is this connection of sickness and sin that motivates James to say, "And the prayer offered in faith will make the sick person well; the Lord will raise him up. *If he has sinned, he will be forgiven*" (James 5:15, emphasis added).

The perspective of the biblical writer of the connection of sin and sickness is further clarified when he goes on to say in the next verse: "Therefore confess your sins to each other and pray for each other so that you may be healed" (5:16). Jesus first forgave the sins of the paralytic before He healed him (Luke 5:20). The reason the psalmist makes the following couplet "who forgives all your sins and heals all your diseases" is because sin is a direct cause of sicknesses, and healing comes only by addressing the cause (Psalm 103:3). Obviously, the cross of Jesus Christ is a must when seeking healing for diseases caused by sin, because only Jesus' cross solves the sin problem.

It was only nine months from the time of writing this article that I was healed from a long-existing stomach problem according to the instructions of James 5. The sickness was caused by my eating habits that were shaped by gluttony. My healing revealed a need to change my eating habits, thereby encouraging me to forsake my sin. The work of the cross dealt with the cause, while the healing touch of God cured the results of sin upon my body. It was a double cure as is the case of every person when healed of sin-related sickness.

## The Activity of the Devil

The Scriptures make clear that the Evil One is also in the business of causing people to be sick. It was the devil that gave Job his boils. It was a legion of demons that made the man of Gerasene insane. In the Gospels demons are credited with the cause of many physical problems. The woman who was crippled for eighteen years was said to be crippled by a spirit. In spite of the many instances of demonically caused sicknesses in the Bible, we hesitate to approach healing generally from a deliverance perspective lest we be labeled extreme. However, if our illnesses are caused by satanic powers, then there will be no healing apart from deliverance from the oppression of the devil.

It is the cross of Jesus Christ that has disarmed principalities and powers (Colossians 2:15), and it empowers God's saints to cast out demons in Jesus' name. Jesus came to defeat the work of the devil (1 John 3:8), and illness is one of his works. It is the power of the cross that is directly applied to the sufferer of demonic forces that delivers the individual and with that release causes healing.

Concurrent with the rise of the occult in America has come a growing number of ailments that have a demonic cause. It is therefore more common today to observe people with a healing ministry using some form of exorcism. I witnessed exorcism being practiced in a healing service this past year in the church I pastor. While some people took offense that they were thought to be demonized, the most dramatic cures were among those whose problem was identified as demonic. What used to be thought of as the approach of last resort is gaining acceptance as being a common cause of physical ailments and, therefore, receives attention early when considering a diagnosis.

It is the cross work of Jesus that defeats the devil, thus making the atoning work of Jesus a most direct means of finding healing when it is used to exorcise demons.

## The Strategy for Battle

While the cross of Jesus Christ has application to the sources of the curse, sin or the devil, one cannot use the cross in some magical formula to cure all ills. The work of the cross is applied by faith to the need of the moment, and for faith to be operative, the one believing needs to know the specifics of the cause. Faith responds to facts, and faith is difficult to be formed in the absence of truth. As in the medical world, so in the spiritual world, the diagnosis precedes the cure. Therefore, the mystery of the cause of sicknesses often needs to be penetrated as a prelude to the exercise of faith.

All the above can be thought of as the strategy for battle. When God led His people into battle in the Old Testament, He gave them a strategy to win the battle. Victory was dependent upon the correct unfolding of the strategy. In the area of healing, a cure is often not experienced because the battle for healing is not fought according to God's plan of attack.

Strategy needs to be based upon the nature and power of the enemy. The spiritual weapons related to the cross remain the same, but the use of them is determined by the appropriate response. Spiritual warfare should begin first by seeking counsel from God for a strategy that will prove victorious. Unfortunately we approach healing most often in the dark, and we credit the will of God for our failure to see healing.

Our weapons have not lost their power nor God His desire to heal. A faith that sees the power of the cross to heal is a faith that is also willing to tarry before the throne until instructions are given. Whatever the outcome, let's not blame our tools. The cross saves to the uttermost, and that includes the needs of the body.

# The Cross of Jesus Christ and His Return

*by William R. Goetz*

We would be hard pressed to find a single portion of Scripture that more succinctly encapsulates the lifestyle God desires for His children in the light of the return of Jesus Christ than Titus 2:11-14:

> For the grace of God that brings salvation has appeared to all men. It teaches us to say "No" to ungodliness and worldly passions, and to live self-controlled, upright and godly lives in this present age, *while we wait for the blessed hope—the glorious appearing of our great God and Savior*, Jesus Christ, who gave himself for us to redeem us from all wickedness and to purify for himself a people that are his very own, eager to do what is good. (emphasis added)

This passage makes it clear that while we wait for the appearing of Jesus Christ, we are to live both negatively and positively.

Negatively, we are to say "no" to ungodliness and worldly passions. Other Scriptures, such as First Timothy 6:9-10, and Second Timothy 2:22, add to the definition of the negative that is to be avoided. The desire to be rich and the evil desires of youth are indicated as ungodliness from which we are to flee.

Positively, we are to pursue righteousness, godliness, faith, love, endurance, gentleness and peace (1 Timothy 6:11; 2 Timothy 2:22). The Titus passage summarizes these directives by describing the believer's lifestyle as he properly awaits Christ's return in three areas of relationship that fully cover all of life. To live positively is to have a right relationship with oneself—"self-controlled"; with others—"upright"; and with God—"godly."

That such a negative and positive life requires the death to self, which only the cross can accomplish, is a given. Unless the self-life has been put to death, it will conspire with the world and the devil to desire—rather than to flee—riches, the lust of the eyes, the boasting of what one has and does and the cravings of sinful man (1 John 2:16). The pursuit of righteousness, godliness, love, faith, gentleness and peace, on the other hand, is not a characteristic of the uncrucified self-life. Thus, only the work of the cross can enable the kind of negative and positive life we are to live in the anticipation of Christ's coming.

What does such a life look like in the three basic relationships of life?

## My Relationship to Myself: Self-Control

The Greek word *sophronos*, which describes the proper relationship believers are to have with themselves, is variously translated as "self-controlled," "sober," "sound mind." It means to think properly about oneself, with neither pride nor self-degradation.

A.W. Tozer expressed it this way:

> The victorious Christian neither exalts nor downplays himself. His interests have shifted from self to Christ. What he is or is not no longer concerns him. He believes that *he has been crucified with Christ* and is not willing either to praise or deprecate such a man. (emphasis added)

Tozer rightly identifies the cross as the only reason why a Christian can think properly about himself. He wrote:

> Self is the opaque veil that hides the face of God from us. It can be removed only in spiritual experience, never by mere instruction. We may as well try to instruct leprosy out of our system. There must be a work of God in destruction before we are free. *We must invite the cross to do its deadly work within us. We must bring our self-sins to the cross for judgment.* (emphasis added)

Dr. K. Neill Foster, in *Revolution of Love*, pointed out that

> there is a more deceitful enemy [than either Satan or sin]. It is the ogre "self." All too often he is unrecognized and for that reason all the more deadly. It is "the old man." "The flesh." "The carnal nature." There are many names for the big "I." . . .
>
> And what is the answer? [The self] *must die.* "In the same way, count yourselves *dead to sin,* but

alive to God in Christ Jesus. Therefore do not let
sin reign in your mortal body so that you obey its
evil desires." (Romans 6:11-12, emphasis added)

Obviously, only through the cross can we relate to ourselves as God wants us to in the light of Christ's return.

## My Relationship to Others: Uprightness

*Dikaios*, the Greek word for "upright" in Titus 2:12, is
variously translated as "justly," "equitably" and "righ-
teously." It unquestionably means that in all my dealings
with other people—family, neighbors, friends, business
contacts—I am just, fair and upright. And the cross that
brings death to self also brings uprightness to my relationships with others.

Nowhere is this truth more clearly illustrated than in
the many records of spiritual awakenings and revivals in
which the message of the cross has been proclaimed.
When the old nature is put to death by the Spirit, relationships undergo dramatic changes. Marriages are transformed and divorces averted. Family dysfunctions are set
right. Church and neighborhood conflicts are resolved.
Dishonest business practices are forsaken and restitution
made.

In Western Canada in the 1970s a major moving of
the Spirit of God gave birth to a revival movement that
continues some thirty years later. Dr. Erwin Lutzer, who
chronicled that revival in his book, *Flames of Freedom*,
described the initial events:

People [in Saskatoon] had gone to local stores to
return stolen goods, or make up for time they

114

had squandered, or repay those they had cheated. The article listed examples such as a man who admitted to theft who offered to work free of charge to pay for what was taken, another who had defrauded the Workman's Compensation Board confessed and repaid the money, and an employee who paid money into the lunchroom coffee fund for coffee he had taken without paying. Stores and hotels found people returning merchandise or paying for past thefts.

Stories of restitution, confession, and reconciliation are legion. A fifty-year-old unpaid dentist bill was settled; a check for $1,000 sent to a government office to make right a tax cheat; a man who had jumped bail 23 year earlier turned himself in to authorities; merchandise that had been brought into the country illegally was returned to a Customs office, and hundreds of similar accounts.

An "explosion" or a "revolution" of love is how Christian workers in Africa and ordinary people in the Philippines described what happened in their relationships with fellow missionaries or pastors, and with spouses, children, neighbors, business associates and friends, as evangelist K.N. Foster, himself touched by the revival mentioned above, proclaimed the message of the cross with its outworking in death to self.

Without doubt, the application of the cross produces the din of upright relationships with others that God desires His children to demonstrate as they wait for the Lord's return.

## My Relationship to God: Godliness

"Piously," "devoutly," "reverently" are some of the varied translations of the Greek *eusebos*, which in Titus 2:12 is rendered as "godly." To live a godly life, then, is to be in a right and devout relationship with God.

The Scriptures make very clear what that relationship is to be. It is to love God with every power of our entire being—with all our heart, soul, mind and strength, as the Lord Jesus Himself told the inquiring scribe (Mark 12:29-30). This is the first and greatest commandment.

But to love God in this way, while at the same time loving one's self, is an impossibility. Just as one cannot love God and money, as Jesus said, so one cannot love God and self. Unless self has been placed on the cross, unless there has been death to the self-life, there cannot be the love for God described in the first commandment.

Dr. Tozer put it this way:

> In every Christian's heart there is a cross and a throne, and the Christian is on the throne till he puts himself on the cross; if he refuses the cross he remains on the throne. Perhaps this is at the bottom of the backsliding and worldliness among gospel believers today. We want to be saved but we insist that Christ do all the dying. No cross for us, no dethronement, no dying. We remain king within the little kingdom of Mansoul and wear our tinsel crown

with all the pride of a Caesar; but we doom ourselves to the shadows and weakness and spiritual sterility.

Perhaps the experience of Simon Peter is an illustration of the need to die to self in order to love God su-
premely. When he met the Lord after the resurrection
and was asked by Christ "Do you love me?" he could re-
spond only with a friendly *phileo* love. But later, after
Pentecost, he wrote about loving God with *agape* (divine) love, in the context of Christ's coming: "Though
you have not seen [Jesus Christ], you love him" (1 Peter
1:8). The cross, which tradition tells us Peter later embraced literally, makes all the difference.

## In Summary

The Spirit of God, through the Apostle Paul's letter to
Titus, says that while we wait for the blessed hope we
are to say "no" to ungodliness and worldly passions and
"yes" to lives that are characterized by right relationships with ourselves, with those around us and with our
God. To relate to ourselves in these ways demands that
self be put to death.

As Tozer has said, the cross on the hill must become
the cross in our hearts. It must become subjective, in-
ternal and experiential. Death to self is the doorway to
life in the Spirit, as Paul declared in Romans 8:2:
"Through Christ Jesus the law of the Spirit of life set me
free from the law of sin and death."

When the cross becomes experiential, then and only
then is it possible to be right in all the relationships of

life and in that condition to truly long for His appearing. Indeed, the cross unquestionably does have a bearing on our proper preparation for, and anticipation of, the return of our Lord. Even so, come Lord Jesus.

# Participating Authors

NOTE: All of the authors are related to The Christian and Missionary Alliance. They are presented here in the order of their essays.

*Dr. A.W. Tozer* was the beloved editor of *Alliance Life* magazine for many years and the author of more than forty books. He pastored Alliance churches in Chicago and Toronto prior to his death in 1963.

*Dr. Peter N. Nanfelt* is the president of the U.S. Christian and Missionary Alliance.

*Dr. Donald A. Wiggins* is vice president for National Church Ministries of the U.S. Christian and Missionary Alliance.

*Mr. Stephen K. Bailey*, currently on home assignment, serves with CAMA Services in Laos.

*Dr. Arnold L. Cook*, a former president of the Canadian Alliance, is president of the Alliance World Fellowship.

*Dr. Rockwell L. Dillaman* is senior pastor of Allegheny Center Alliance Church in Pittsburgh, PA.

*Rev. Fred A. Hartley III* is pastor of Lilburn Alliance Church in Lilburn, GA.

*Dr. David E. Schroeder* is president of Alliance Theological Seminary and of Nyack College in Nyack, NY.

*Dr. Gerald E. McGraw* is a professor at Toccoa Falls College in Toccoa Falls, GA.

*Miss Lisa M. Rohrick* is a C&MA missionary in Benin, West Africa.

*Rev. Robert B. Goldenberg* is pastor of Circle Drive Alliance Church in Sidney, NY.

*Mr. Douglas B. Wicks* is the publisher of Christian Publications, Inc., in Camp Hill, PA.

*Dr. John A. Harvey* is pastor of First Alliance Church in Toccoa, GA.

*Dr. William R. Goetz* is a retired pastor and author living in Linden, AB, Canada.

# *Other Voices Books*

*Prayer Voices*
*Holiness Voices*
*Missionary Voices*
*Voices on the Glory*
*Church-Planting Voices*
*Healing Voices*
*Voices from a Changing America*
*Voices on the Family*